JULIUS CAESAR
THE 1-HOUR GUIDEBOOK

AN ILLUSTRATED GUIDE FOR MASTERING
SHAKESPEARE'S GREAT POLITICAL EPIC

David Grey & Gigi Bach, editors

SPARK PUBLISHING

This edition published by Spark Publishing
in agreement with Bermond Press.

SPARKNOTES is a registered trademark of SparkNotes, LLC.

Spark Publishing
120 Fifth Avenue
New York, NY 10011

Printed in the United States of America

10 9 8 7 6 5 4 3 2 1

ISBN 1-4114-0449-1
Library of Congress Catalog-in-Publication Data available on request.

Cover and book design by Dreamedia, Inc.

NEW & UPCOMING TITLES

IN THE 1-HOUR GUIDEBOOK SERIES

Hamlet
Romeo & Juliet
Macbeth
A Midsummer Night's Dream
Othello

CONTENTS

ACKNOWLEDGEMENTS

The editors would like to extend our warmest gratitude to the following people who supported us with their encouragement, feedback, proofreading and inspiration: Barbara, David and Beverly, Lisa, Brian, Professor Louis A. Montrose, Professor Emeritus Robert McCoy and Sterling Professor Harold Bloom.

FOREWORD

This book emerged from our desire to provide the unfamiliar reader with the most comprehensive, clear picture of Shakespeare's *Julius Caesar* in the least amount of time. In addition, our awe of Shakespeare's work nurtured a passion to present the information in a way that complemented the greatness of his work. Why shouldn't the beauty of a Shakespeare primer at least attempt to mirror the beauty of the subject? Briefly stated, why does a literary guidebook have to look ugly? The obvious answer is that it doesn't, especially when illustration collaborating with text is the best way to accomplish our desire for clarity and quick assimilation. Neither text nor graphics is exclusive to the brain. We think in pictures; we think in words. The cognitive interaction between the two is the quickest path to understanding.

When developing a picture of our audience, therefore, we held these characteristics foremost: frightening lack of time, need for clarity, desire for beauty.

Certain innovations arose in attempting to satisfy this model—visual distillations, plot timelines, dramatic maps, quick reviews of the characters, scene by scene illustrations and more. By the same criteria, certain traditional elements were eliminated—you won't, for example, find lengthy commentary in this book. Most of the commentary we have found in other study guides to Shakespeare was either overly obvious or arguably incorrect. To take up valuable time with our own commentary would be counter to our purpose, which we felt demanded concrete summary rather than questionable surmise.

As far as our specific decisions regarding *Julius Caesar,* at every opportunity we tried to convey some sense of the internal struggle of Marcus Brutus. He is at once warring against Cassius' pragmatic realism that would destroy his idealistic principles, Caesar's ambition that would destroy his beloved republic and his own dark motivations that would allow his stoic nobility to harbor thoughts of murder.

That Shakespeare sought to explore this conflicted world of the rational idealist—the moral murderer—would, of course, serve him later in the construction of *Hamlet*. Portia attempts to penetrate the veil of this world, with little success beyond praise and promises to change. Brutus has little success, himself, with his internal conflict, ultimately producing the psychological specter of Caesar's spirit. Octavius, in some sense a fusion between the rational Brutus and the pragmatic Cassius, would later sidestep the dilemma altogether and maintain a working dictatorship under the guise of an idealized republic.

We attempted to paint Caesar as neither a good nor a bad man, as both judgments are far too narrow for the colossus of Rome. He is, instead, shown for what Shakespeare shows him to be: a leader of competence and weakness, ego and humanity, who is responding to the exigencies of a young empire. Contradictory traits are not unique to Caesar or Brutus. The inclusion of a chapter on "Building Character" was introduced to examine this thought in more detail.

Our scene by scene summaries normally give equal, single-page weight to each scene division. The disproportionate scene length in this play was a constant difficulty; it was not without much reflection that we combined 4.2 and the first part of 4.3 (the argument), leaving the final part of 4.3 (the reconciliation) to its own page. We ask your indulgence.

Congratulations on your adventure into Shakespeare's inimitable masterwork.

David Grey & Gigi Bach, editors

Th. Equidem malorum maximum hunc cumulum reor,
si abominanda casus optanda efficit.
Nvn. Et si odia seruas, cur madent fletu genae?
Th. Quod interemi, non quod amisi, fleo.

THESEUS: This is the very summit of calamity,
When Fate makes us demand what we must loathe.
MESSENGER: If you still harbor hate, why do you weep?
THESEUS: I weep, not that I lost, but that I killed him.

Seneca
Phaedra (1116-1119)

Caesar's
circle

Caesar's inner circle consists of the imperator himself, along with two politically-astute men who struggle against the conspirators after the assassination. Caesar is portrayed as a complex character—at once majestic and human—whose grand presence brings about the conflicting goods of a benevolent monarchy against a republic. Antony shoulders the burden of the post-assassination counter-movement against the conspirators, manipulating the fickle Roman public to anarchy with his brilliant funeral oration. Octavius, who historically shoulders the burden of empire, is painted as being almost above consequence (no one in his family makes it onto the death proscripion), and as such, he is a foil to Brutus' looming reckoning.

COWARDS DIE

many times before their deaths.
The valiant never taste of death but once.
Of all the wonders that I yet have heard,
It seems to me most strange that men should fear,
Seeing that death, a necessary end,
Will come when it will come.

2.2.32-37

THIS IS CAESAR

HE IS BY FAR THE MOST powerful man in the Roman Empire and—while Brutus is the central figure of this tragedy—Caesar's assassination and funeral will be the two central events of the play.

Caesar is first seen as a victorious general, having just returned from his conquest over the sons of his ally-turned-rival, Pompey, in Spain. Caesar returns to a Rome housing an emerging faction wary of his growing power and its threat to the republic.

ET TU

BRUTÉ?

The force of Caesar's character is such that all other characters may be examined in light of their relationship to him: Antony is loyal, Cassius is jealous, Brutus is conflicted, Calpurnia is worried, Casca is disgusted, Octavius is indifferent. Shakespeare skillfully paints a portrait of a man who is both colossus and human and who, in the end, is deserving of all these disparate sentiments.

QUESTION
Shakespeare shows Caesar as an egotistical, power-hungry monarch and as a thoughtful, benevolent ruler. This dichotomy gives rise to the deliberately unresolved question: Is Caesar's assassination murder or tyrannicide?

GHOST
The ghost of Caesar appears to Brutus twice in the play: once at Sardis and once at Philippi. The ghost—an ominous reminder that the degenerating state of affairs following the assassination are Brutus' own doing—identifies himself only as, "thy evil spirit, Brutus."

FRIENDS, ROMANS,

countrymen, lend me your ears.
I come to bury Caesar, not to praise him.
The evil that men do lives after them;
The good is oft interred with their bones.
So let it be with Caesar.

3.2.71-75

QUESTION
What two events mark the climactic center of the play? (ANSWER ON PAGE 18)

THIS IS MARK ANTONY

HE IS CAESAR'S CLOSEST political ally and friend. Antony is athletic and a reveler. Whenever he is with Caesar, they always seem to share a close, intimate communication or a joke.

Antony offers Caesar a crown three times at the games (the moment is staged by them to gauge the crowd's reaction to his kingship) and Caesar rejects it, each time less forcefully. Afterward, Caesar confides in Antony that he is wary of Cassius (who, unknown to them both, is forming a conspiracy to assassinate Caesar).

CRY HAVOC

Antony speaks at Caesar's funeral, cleverly convincing the fickle crowd (they have just called for Brutus to be crowned) that the conspirators should pay with their lives. In doing so, Antony appropriates a great deal of the tenderness by which we view Brutus' thoughtful character and replaces our affectionate view with one of critical skepticism. Antony's funeral oration is one of the greatest moments in all of Shakespearean theater.

PRETENSE
After the assassination, Antony pretends to befriend and respect the conspirators, shaking each of their bloody hands. Later, however, Antony shows that he is only attempting to gain Brutus' permission to speak at the funeral, thus gaining a platform from which to influence the crowd.

TRIUMVIR
Antony, along with Octavius and Lepidus, is a member of the emerging triumvirate following Caesar's assassination. He contends with the contrarian Octavius (who is as consummate a politician as Antony is a general) and the two men lead armies against the conspirators.

ACCORDING TO HIS VIRTUE

let us use him,
With all respect and rites of burial.
Within my tent his bones tonight shall lie
Most like a soldier, ordered honorably.
So call the field to rest, and let's away
To part the glories of this happy day.

5.5.76-81

ANSWER
Julius Caesar's assassination and funeral mark the climactic center of the play.

QUESTION
What does Mark Antony present Caesar with at the Lupercal games? (ANSWER ON PAGE 21)

THIS IS CAESAR'S
YOUNG HEIR

CAESAR'S GRAND-NEPHEW and heir, Octavius is not seen in the play until after the climactic assassination and funeral oration. The consummate politician, Octavius is preoccupied with nothing if not building his power base.

Octavius is first seen with Antony and Lepidus constructing the death proscriptions of 100 senators. His cool aloofness sets him apart from either of the two triumvirs, dispossessed of Antony's sensuality or Lepidus' cooperative nature.

I WILL
DO SO

Octavius contradicts Antony's military suggestions, leading the action on the right flank against Brutus' forces. His army suffers an early defeat at Brutus' hand, but serendipitous events allow Antony to encircle Cassius, who commits a premature suicide. After the victory over the conspirators, Octavius accepts all of Brutus' loyal men into his own service.

HISTORY
Shakespeare does not mention the historical struggle between Antony and Octavius in the early formation of the second triumvirate, which took 20 months from the assassination of Caesar to ratify. He does, however, show glimpses of friction between them whenever they are together.

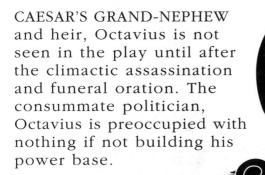

Julius Caesar
RULER OF ROME

Characterized as a political colossus, Caesar's rising power and growing ambition are viewed by some as a threat to the republic. His grandeur is tempered by a list of physical infirmities, including hearing loss and epilepsy. Blinded to the warnings of others by his own imperial stature, Caesar is brutally assassinated at the midpoint of the play. Antony's oration at Caesar's funeral begins the countermovement against the conspirators. Caesar's ghost haunts Brutus until his suicide.

laurel wreath

friend and political ally   *grand-nephew and heir*

Antony
EMERGING TRIUMVIR

Caesar's closest political ally, Antony presents
a crown three times to Caesar at the Lupercal
games (the moment is presumably staged).
After Caesar's assassination, Antony pretends
to befriend the conspirators, but does so only
to gain permission to speak at the funeral. He
brilliantly uses the public forum to turn the
crowd against the conspirators. Along with
Octavius, Antony leads armies against the
conspirators at Philippi, defeating Cassius in
the first battle and Brutus in the second.

Octavius
EMERGING TRIUMVIR

Not seen until after the funeral of Caesar,
Octavius is characterized as politically deft
and personally aloof. He constructs the
proscription of 100 senators with Lepidus and
Antony. Ignoring Antony's suggestion,
Octavius leads the legions on the right wing
against the army of Brutus at Philippi, where
he is initially defeated. After the decisive
victory in the second battle, Octavius accepts
all of Brutus' loyal men into his own service.

general's helmet

eagle of rome

ANSWER Mark Antony presents Caesar with a laurel crown (which Caesar rejects three times) at the Lupercal games.

Architects
of *the*
conspiracy

*Examined in light of their basic
motivations, Cassius is envious of
Caesar's power, while Brutus is fearful
of its danger to the republic. Brutus has
by far the more intellectual struggle,
making him the central figure of the
tragedy. He is a type of the moral
criminal—specifically, a man who
is considering murder as an
ethical imperative. Cassius will be
the overruled voice of pragmatism,
especially in decisions regarding
Mark Antony—a man he well
understands. Last, Casca
is all Brutus strives to
avoid with the conspiracy:
he is duplicitous, self-
affecting and not above
stabbing from behind.*

IT MUST BE

by his death, and for my part
I know no personal cause to spurn at him
But for the general. He would be crowned.

2.1.10-13

QUESTION
What is Octavius' relationship to Caesar? (ANSWER ON PAGE 26)

THIS IS BRUTUS

HE IS THE CENTRAL figure of the play and, as such, his dilemma becomes its chief concern: *Is it right to commit murder to guard against a future threat to the republic?*

Brutus is seduced into the conspiracy by Cassius, who needs Brutus' noble reputation to lend credibility to his cause. Because Brutus is an intellective idealist, he must construct—going so far as to invent—the case against Caesar in his mind (the pivotal garden soliloquy). From that point on, Brutus takes the lead role in the assassination conspiracy.

AN HONORABLE MAN

After the funeral oration riots, Brutus discovers he is unable to control the countless variables that comprise the unintended consequences of his idealistic actions: for example, killing Caesar without a plan to seize control, safeguarding a political threat, then providing the threat with a public forum. He rushes into battle at Philippi (against Cassius' better judgment) and commits suicide rather than suffer shame.

CONSEQUENCE

Peripeteia is a sudden turn of events in which an action has an antithetical consequence to its intention. Brutus, who watches helplessly as Caesar's assassination transforms Rome from an imperiled republic into a riotous mobocracy, is haunted by his ghost—the personified figure of Brutus' own folly.

COMPLICATION

Shakespeare makes no mention of the historical gossip that Brutus was Caesar's illegitimate child (while the relationship was most likely untrue, Caesar did have a well-known affair with Brutus' mother). Shakespeare does not complicate their relationship, though it may have motivated the dying remark, "Et tu, Bruté?" Brutus was also rumored to have stabbed Caesar in the groin, which leads to its own set of paternal resonances.

...THIS FEARFUL NIGHT

There is no stir or walking in the streets,
And the complexion of the element
In favor's like the work we have in hand,
Most bloody, fiery, and most terrible.

1.3.127-131

ANSWER
Octavius is Caesar's grand-nephew and chosen heir.

QUESTION
What reason does Brutus give for assassinating Caesar? (ANSWER ON PAGE 28)

THIS IS CASSIUS

HE IS THE BROTHER-IN-LAW of Brutus and the key figure in planning the assassination. In Act One, he lobbies for Brutus to lead the conspiracy, hoping Brutus' noble reputation will lend credibility to the cause.

Not sharing in Brutus' moral bewilderment, Cassius' directness and pragmatism are a sharp contrast to Brutus' intellectual idealism. Not above subterfuge, Cassius forges letters from citizens pleading for Brutus' leadership and has the messages anonymously delivered.

A LEAN
AND HUNGRY LOOK

After the first battle at Philippi, Cassius—ever the pessimist—leaps to the conclusion that his army has been overrun (it is really Brutus' men he sees in the distance, come to deliver the good news that they have defeated Octavius). Cassius has his servant assist in his suicide, dying with the words, "Caesar, thou art revenged, / Even with the sword that killed thee."

ENVY
While Brutus seems genuinely concerned that Roman rule by a senatorial body may collapse under the weight of Caesar's monarchical ambition, Cassius appears to be motivated by simple spite and envy. When first lobbying for Brutus' involvement, Cassius proclaims, "The fault, dear Brutus is not in our stars, / But in ourselves, that we are underlings."

JUDGMENT
After securing Brutus' involvement, Cassius defers to his brother-in-law's judgment, to the downfall of the conspiracy. Brutus, in a cascade of strategic errors, safeguards Antony from harm, provides him with a public forum and rushes to meet him in battle at Philippi—each time against the better judgment of Cassius.

YOU SPEAK TO CASCA,

and to such a man
That is no fleering telltale. Hold, my hand.
Be factious for redress of all these griefs,
And I will set this foot of mine as far
As who goes farthest.

1.3.117-121

ANSWER
Brutus justifies the assassination by reasoning that Caesar is a future threat to the republic.

QUESTION
What underhanded tactic does Cassius employ to enlist Brutus in his cause? (ANSWER ON PAGE 31)

THIS IS CASCA

CASCA IS A POLITICIAN of Rome and a member of the inner circle surrounding Caesar. Casca is hallmarked by pretense: he at first appears to be attentive to Caesar, but later speaks of him in tones of disgust and contempt.

Casca is referred to as dull or stupid by both Brutus and Cassius. Cassius, however, qualifies the assessment, saying Casca is merely pretending to be dull—but is sharp in matters of importance.

SPEAK, HANDS, FOR ME!

Casca meets the others at Caesar's house to escort him to the senate. Once at the senate house, the conspirators close tightly around Caesar, pretending to second a petition brought before him, while Casca sneaks behind him. As Caesar rebuffs their entreaties, Casca leaps up and stabs Caesar in the back of the neck—the first of thirty-three deadly blows.

COWARD
Casca is portrayed as cowardly: he is afraid to open his mouth at the Lupercal games, for fear he will breathe the stench of the crowd; he is fearful of the storm and the unnatural occurrences in 1.3; he stabs Caesar in the back. Casca is not seen in the play after the assassination.

FORESHADOW
Casca details the events of Caesar's epilepsy—a dramatic foreshadowing of the assassination. At one point, Casca says Caesar offered his throat to the cheering crowd before fainting. Casca admits he was tempted to take Caesar up on his offer.

politician and conspirator

Brutus
INTELLECTIVE IDEALIST

A noble idealist who convinces himself
Caesar must be assassinated because he
may be a future threat to the republic.
Leads the conspiracy from Act Two onward.
He is the husband of Portia, who desires his
confidence. Brutus' decision to spare
Antony, to allow him to speak at Caesar's
funeral and to rush into battle against him
at Philippi guarantee the end of the
conspirators. He commits suicide after his
defeat in the second battle at Philippi.

dove and arrow

politician and conspirator   *politician and conspirator*

Cassius

CONVINCES BRUTUS TO JOIN

The brother-in-law of Brutus, Cassius is the key figure in the development of the conspiracy. He convinces Brutus to join, using underhanded tactics—forging letters and placing them where Brutus will find them. After the assassination, Cassius switches from a villainous figure to a tragic one. Against his better judgment, Cassius gives in to Brutus' cascade of poor decisions involving Antony. Cassius' one misjudgment after the first battle at Philippi leads to his own suicide.

Casca

FIRST TO STAB CAESAR

Member of Caesar's inner circle, Casca at first appears to be attentive to the Roman leader. Later, however, his words betray an attitude of disdain and disgust. Casca relates the story of Caesar's fall at the Lupercal games, after the staged rejection of the crown offered by Antony. Casca is called dim-witted, but Cassius qualifies it, saying it is a pretense for social acceptance. Casca stabs Caesar in the back of the neck, initiating the assassination.

forged letters

two-faced

ANSWER Cassius forges letters from the citizens of Rome calling for Brutus' leadership and has them anonymously delivered to Brutus.

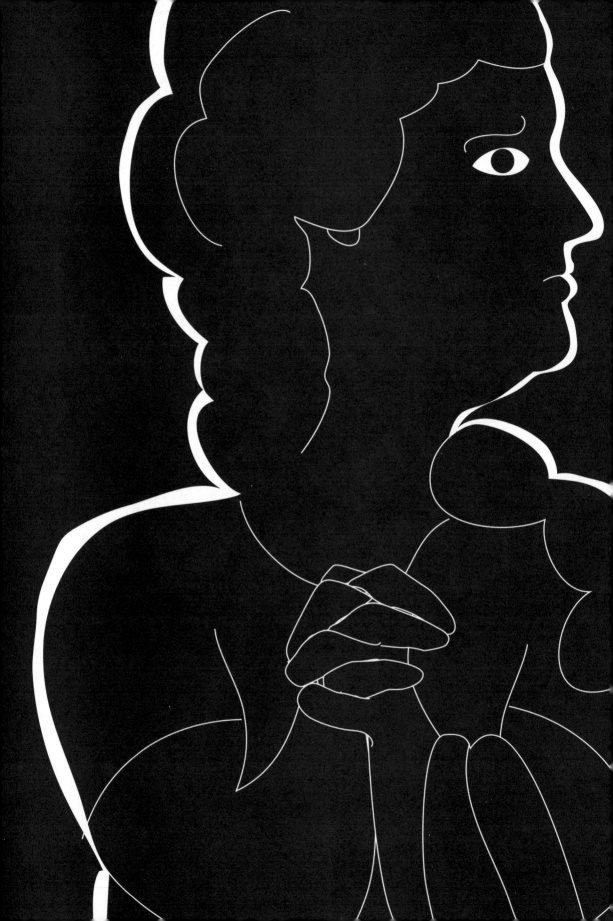

The
two wives

The wives of the two protagonists serve to highlight the dramatic tension of the assassination. Calpurnia's logical argument for Caesar to abstain from the senate—she cites natural, supernatural and personal support—is first heeded and then discarded (Decius' flattery proves more effective). Portia's emotional appeal to be taken into Brutus' confidence is one of the most touching scenes in the play, followed powerfully by her frantic sending of Lucius on the ambiguous errand to the senate house. As voices of reason in a dramatic tragedy, the wives' efforts must, of course, be frustrated in the end.

WHEN BEGGARS DIE

there are no comets seen.
The heavens themselves blaze forth the death of princes.

2.2.30-31

QUESTION

Who is the first conspirator to stab Caesar? (ANSWER ON PAGE 36)

THIS IS
CALPURNIA

SHE IS CAESAR'S WIFE, who shows genuine concern for him, despite Caesar's dismissive attitude toward her. Calpurnia's first appearance is telling, as Caesar bellows for her on the way to the Lupercalia.

When she finally comes forward (she was obviously not alongside Caesar), it is to answer obediently, "Here, my Lord." Caesar then orders her to stand where Antony can touch her during the fertility race—which rather directly focuses the blame for his lack of an heir on her (Caesar is fifty-six at the time).

DO NOT
GO FORTH TODAY

The night before the assassination, Calpurnia calls out three times in her sleep, "Help, ho! They murder Caesar!" She speaks to Caesar in the morning, warning him of the reported strange occurrences (graves opening, the sky raining blood, etc.). Caesar tells Decius that his wife dreamt he was a fountain, spouting blood for Romans to wash their hands in. Decius reinterprets the dream with a flattering spin and Caesar disregards Calpurnia's concerns, regretting he was ever swayed by them.

CASSANDRA
Portia, Brutus' wife, also shares a genuine concern for her husband. Portia's concern, however, is more pressingly communicated as a desire for intimacy. Calpurnia has a simpler role as a type of Cassandra, who foretold the destruction of Troy, but was not believed.

HISTORY
Calpurnia is the historic third and final wife of Julius Caesar. Although in the play Mark Antony says he found Caesar's will in the late ruler's closet, Plutarch reveals that Calpurnia actually delivered it to Antony after Caesar's murder.

TELL ME YOUR COUNSELS,

I will not disclose 'em.
I have strong proof of my constancy,
Giving myself a voluntary wound
Here in the thigh. Can I bear that with patience,
And not my husband's secrets?

2.1.300-304

ANSWER
Casca is the first conspirator to act, stabbing Caesar from behind.

QUESTION
How is Caesar represented in Calpurnia's dream? (ANSWER ON PAGE 39)

THIS IS BRUTUS' WIFE

HER NAME IS PORTIA and she is the daughter of the Roman philosopher Cato. Although she appears in only two scenes in the play, her lines are among the most passionate uttered by a female Shakespearean character.

Portia's first appearance is with Brutus after the other conspirators have gone home. Sensing that something is weighing heavily on Brutus, she pleads with him to take her into his confidence. She reveals a self-inflicted wound on her thigh, which she bore in secret to prove her steadfast loyalty. Brutus is moved, but is interrupted before he can confide in her.

TRUE AND
HONORABLE WIFE

On the day of Caesar's assassination, Portia frantically sends Lucius to the senate house to determine if Brutus is safe. She still knows nothing of the conspiracy—except what her intuition tells her—and her confusion adds to the dramatic tension. At the end of the play, Brutus hears at Sardis that Portia has committed suicide by swallowing hot coals. The horrible news motivates his argument with Cassius.

RELATIONSHIPS
Portia's father was Marcus Porcius Cato Uticencis, also known as Cato the Younger (who strongly opposed Caesar). The Young Cato in Shakespeare's play is actually his son—Portia and Shakespeare's Young Cato were siblings. To complicate matters further, Brutus' mother, Servilia, was half-sister to Portia's father, making Portia and Brutus first cousins.

Calpurnia
WIFE OF CAESAR

Obedient and submissive, Calpurnia is concerned for her husband's safety. She cites the strange occurrences (natural evidence), the soothsayer's prophecy (supernatural evidence) and her own troubling dream (personal evidence) as reasons for Caesar not to go to the senate house. Caesar at first gives in to her concern, but is later swayed by the flattering reinterpretation of Calpurnia's dream by Decius, one of the conspirators. Calpurnia is not seen after the assassination.

comet

Portia

WIFE OF BRUTUS

Wife and first cousin to Brutus. Sister to Young Cato in the play. Sensing Brutus is troubled, after the meeting of the conspirators, she petitions her husband to be taken into his confidence. She reveals a self-inflicted wound on her thigh that she has suffered in private as proof she will guard his secrets. He is moved to tell her, but is interrupted. When Brutus is at the senate house, Portia sends Lucius on an ambiguous errand to check on him. In Sardis, Brutus hears Portia has died eating hot coals.

hot coals

ANSWER In Calpurnia's dream, Caesar is a fountain with 100 spouts of blood, which many Romans wash their hands in.

A QUICK REVIEW *of*

Julius Caesar

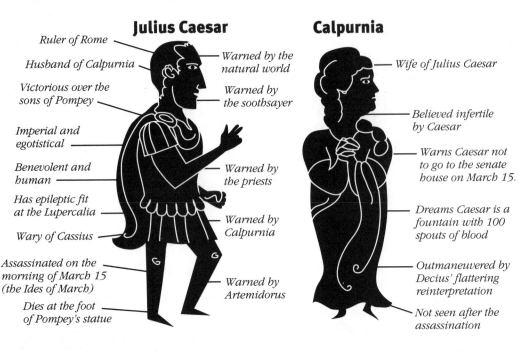

- Ruler of Rome
- Husband of Calpurnia
- Victorious over the sons of Pompey
- Imperial and egotistical
- Benevolent and human
- Has epileptic fit at the Lupercalia
- Wary of Cassius
- Assassinated on the morning of March 15 (the Ides of March)
- Dies at the foot of Pompey's statue
- Warned by the natural world
- Warned by the soothsayer
- Warned by the priests
- Warned by Calpurnia
- Warned by Artemidorus

Calpurnia

- Wife of Julius Caesar
- Believed infertile by Caesar
- Warns Caesar not to go to the senate house on March 15.
- Dreams Caesar is a fountain with 100 spouts of blood
- Outmaneuvered by Decius' flattering reinterpretation
- Not seen after the assassination

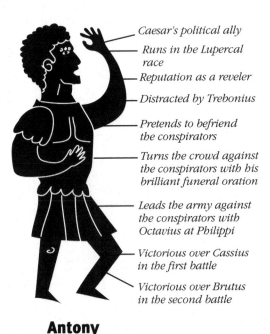

- Caesar's political ally
- Runs in the Lupercal race
- Reputation as a reveler
- Distracted by Trebonius
- Pretends to befriend the conspirators
- Turns the crowd against the conspirators with his brilliant funeral oration
- Leads the army against the conspirators with Octavius at Philippi
- Victorious over Cassius in the first battle
- Victorious over Brutus in the second battle

Antony

- Grand-nephew and heir of Caesar
- Confident and equanimous
- Controls Rome with Antony and Lepidus
- Loses to Brutus in first battle at Philippi
- Wins with Antony in second battle at Philippi
- Takes all of Brutus' loyal followers into his own service

Octavius

THE MAJOR CHARACTERS

Brutus

Roman politician

Stoic philosopher

Cousin and husband of Portia

Noble

Intellective idealist

Leads the conspiracy

Constructs the case for assassination

Decides to spare Antony

Allows Antony to speak at funeral

Commits suicide while retreating from loss at Philippi

Wins first battle at Philippi against Octavius

Loses second battle at Philippi against Antony and Octavius

Portia

Cousin and wife of Brutus

Concerned

Pleads to be taken into Brutus' confidence

Suffers self-inflicted wound on thigh to prove her discretion

Frantically sends Lucius on ambiguous errand to the senate house

Commits suicide by swallowing hot coals

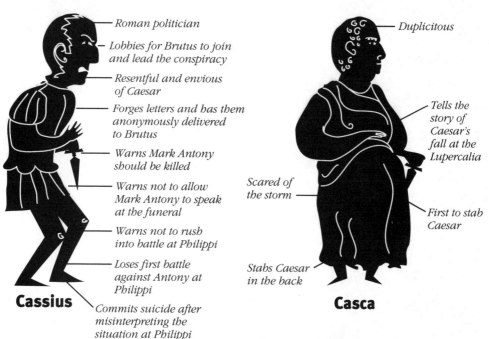

Cassius

Roman politician

Lobbies for Brutus to join and lead the conspiracy

Resentful and envious of Caesar

Forges letters and has them anonymously delivered to Brutus

Warns Mark Antony should be killed

Warns not to allow Mark Antony to speak at the funeral

Warns not to rush into battle at Philippi

Loses first battle against Antony at Philippi

Commits suicide after misinterpreting the situation at Philippi

Casca

Duplicitous

Tells the story of Caesar's fall at the Lupercalia

Scared of the storm

First to stab Caesar

Stabs Caesar in the back

the Minor *characters*

The minor characters play many important roles in Julius Caesar. The secondary conspirators form a political cadre of men bent on the execution of the most powerful man in Rome. The cautioners are foils to Caesar's egotism, in the case of the Soothsayer, and selflessness, in the case of Artemidorus. The fickle plebeians are, in turn, harassed, manipulated and

lied to. The allies form a nexus of loyal compatriots, which is praised by Antony. The senators suffer as a result of political power-grabbing— only Popilius is unharmed. Last, minor servants, such as Lucius and Pindarus, play roles that touch the hearts of their masters.

SET ON YOUR FOOT,

And with a heart new-fired I follow you,
To do I know not what. But it sufficeth
That Brutus leads me on.

2.1.334-337

QUESTION
How does Brutus' wife, Portia, die? (ANSWER ON PAGE 46)

THE SECONDARY CONSPIRATORS

DECIUS

As Caesar is talked into staying home by Calpurnia, Decius arrives to escort him to the senate house. He shrewdly reinterprets Calpurnia's dream, transforming its message into Caesar's nourishment of the people. Decius prompts Caesar into going to the senate by telling him they plan to make him king that morning.

CINNA

During the unnatural storm, Cinna comes upon Cassius and Casca. Cassius gives Cinna the forged letters, telling him to place them in various locations where Brutus will find them. Cinna asks no questions, but does as he is told. After the assassination of Caesar, he is the first to proclaim, "Liberty! Freedom! Tyranny is dead!"

METELLUS

In the meeting at Brutus' house, Metellus recommends they include Ligarius because of a public berating he received from Caesar. Metellus presents his petition to Caesar—the return of his exiled brother—the ruse for bringing the conspirators within stabbing distance.

TREBONIUS

Trebonius, with Brutus, rejects the idea of killing Antony along with Caesar. Trebonius is tasked with removing Antony just prior to the assassination, calling him aside under the pretense of a private discussion.

LIGARIUS

The last conspirator to be added. He is recommended by Metellus because of a public berating he received from Caesar. Ligarius arrives at the home of Brutus, after the meeting has ended, wrapped in a shawl because of an illness. Shakespeare, however, makes it unclear how real the illness is. Brutus commends him for his bravery.

WHEREFORE REJOICE?

What conquest brings he home?
What tributaries follow him to Rome
To grace in captive bonds his chariot wheels?
You blocks, you stones, you worse than senseless things,
O you hard hearts, you cruel men of Rome,
Knew you not Pompey?

1.1.32-37

THE SENATORS

CICERO
Maturity and wisdom

Cicero assigns natural causes to the storm. He is suggested as a conspirator for his maturity and wisdom, but is rejected by Brutus who says Cicero will not follow anything that he has not started himself. Cicero is later executed by order of Antony and Octavius.

PUBLIUS
Confused and afraid

Publius is a senator and Antony's nephew. On the morning of the assassination he appears to escort Caesar to the senate. Immediately after the assassination, Brutus calms Publius, who is standing nearby. Later, Publius' execution is ordered by Antony, Octavius and Lepidus.

POPILIUS LENA
Possible exposure

The morning of the assassination, Popilius expresses to Cassius his wishes for Cassius' success. Moments later he is seen talking with Caesar, causing Cassius to fear their plot is exposed. Brutus then points out Popilius' smile, saying he is not talking about them with Caesar.

THE TRIBUNES

FLAVIUS AND MURELLUS
Angry about Caesar's growing power

Flavius and Murellus open the play with an interrogation of some common workers on their way to pay tribute to Caesar. The two officials are incensed that the same people who cheered Pompey would now cheer Caesar for his victory over that great general's sons. They disburse the crowds, then remove decorations from the statues celebrating Caesar. They are later punished for this.

CAESAR, BEWARE

*of Brutus. Take heed of Cassius.
Come not near Casca. Have an eye to Cinna. Trust not
Trebonius. Mark well Metellus Cimber. Decius
Brutus loves thee not. Thou hast wronged Caius
Ligarius. There is but one mind in all these men, and
It is bent against Caesar.*

2.3.1-6

ANSWER
Decius, one of the conspirators, convinces Caesar to go to the senate house on March 15.

QUESTION
Who speaks to Caesar, causing Cassius to fear their assassination plot is exposed? (ANSWER ON PAGE 50)

THE CAUTIONERS

SOOTHSAYER
"Beware the Ides of March"

After delivering his famous warning to Caesar during the Lupercalia festival, Caesar dismisses him as a dreamer. The Soothsayer reappears the morning of the assassination. Just before Caesar enters the senate house, he calls to the Soothsayer, "The Ides of March have come." The Soothsayer replies, "Ay, Caesar, but not gone."

ARTEMIDORUS
A letter of warning

A teacher of rhetoric, Artemidorus pens a letter of warning to Caesar, naming all eight conspirators. In the press of the crowd, Artemidorus hands the letter to Caesar and urges him to read it immediately, telling him it concerns Caesar personally. Caesar brushes it off, saying magnanimously that what touches him personally shall be attended to last.

THE POETS

CINNA THE POET AND ANOTHER POET
Victims

After Antony's impassioned funeral speech, the mob is incited against the conspirators. Cinna the poet has the unfortunate coincidence of having the same name as Cinna the conspirator. Even after he convinces the mob that he is not the same Cinna, they still kill him for "bad verses." The second poet admonishes Brutus and Cassius during their long argument and is insultingly dismissed by Brutus as having nothing to do with the war.

SAFE, ANTONY,

Brutus is safe enough.
I dare assure thee that no enemy
Shall ever take alive the noble Brutus.
The gods defend him from so great a shame!
When you do find him, or alive or dead,
He will be found like Brutus, like himself.

5.3.20-25

ANSWER
Popilius wishes Cassius success, then speaks with Caesar, leading Cassius to believe
their assassination plot has been exposed.

QUESTION
Why doesn't Caesar read Artemidorus' letter naming the conspirators? (ANSWER ON PAGE 52)

THE ALLIES

LUCILIUS AND MESSALA
Close friends of Brutus

When he is captured by Antony's soldiers, Lucilius tells them he is Brutus. His ruse is discovered by Antony who treats him with kindness. Messala brings Brutus up to date on events back in Rome. He is with Titinius when Cassius is discovered dead. In the end, he recommends Strato to Octavius.

TITINIUS
Cassius' best friend

During the final battle, Titinius is sent by Cassius to determine if the troops near his tents are friends or enemies. Viewing the activity, Pindarus misreads what is happening and tells Cassius that Titinius has been taken. In soliloquy Titinius relates that he met with allies and that Cassius has misconstrued everything, killing himself needlessly. He lays a victory wreath from Brutus on Cassius' head, then stabs himself with Cassius' sword.

YOUNG CATO
Portia's brother • Brave soldier

At the discovery of Titinius death shortly after that of Cassius', Cato, Portia's brother, points out to Brutus and Messala that Titinius placed the victory wreath on Cassius' head. Later, when Brutus urges his soldiers on in battle, Cato responds bravely, proclaiming his name and his patriotism in the field. He is killed by soldiers of Antony and Octavius.

VOLUMNIUS
Longtime friend

Brutus pleads with Volumnius to hold his sword, thereby assisting him in his suicide. He tells Volumnius that he saw the ghost of Caesar, proving his time is near. Pressing the matter, Brutus cites their childhood friendship, but Volumnius gently refuses, saying it is not an occupation for a friend.

LABEO AND FLAVIUS,

set our battles on.
'Tis three o'clock; and, Romans, yet ere night
We shall try fortune in a second fight.

5.3.109-111

THE SOLDIERS

VARRO AND CLAUDIUS
Chief officers of Brutus

Varro and Claudius are asleep in Brutus' tent when the ghost of Caesar first appears to Brutus. After the ghost is gone, Brutus wakes the two men and asks if they cried out in their sleep. The sleepy officers reply that they are unsure, but that they saw nothing. Brutus sends them to Cassius with orders to advance his army.

THREE MORE SOLDIERS
For Brutus and Cassius

The three soldiers, although they speak no lines in the play, are employed to fill out the armies of Brutus and Cassius. Used interchangeably in either general's service, the soldiers, nevertheless are not present at the end of the play when Brutus urges the remainder of his friends to rest. This gives visual credibility to the loss of Brutus' army in the battle.

LABEO AND FLAVIUS
Officers in the war

When Brutus is taken to see the body of Cassius, that of Titinius is also found. Brutus, nearly defeated, calls Labeo and Flavius to advance the troops. These two men are likely officers in Brutus' army, taken from the context of the order and their proximity to Brutus. They have no lines in the play, but add to the sense of a large army fighting in battle.

TWO SOLDIERS OF ANTHONY
Fooled by Lucilius

In the midst of battle, Lucilius, confronted by two of Antony's soldiers, offers them money to kill him, saying they will be killing Brutus. The first soldier says they must not, as Brutus is an important prisoner. They bring the news to Antony. Antony easily spots the ruse and orders the two soldiers to take Lucilius and treat him kindly.

TRULY, SIR,

*all that I live by is with the awl. I meddle with no
tradesman's matters nor women's matters, but withal I am
indeed, sir, a surgeon to old shoes. When they are in great
danger, I recover them. As proper men as ever trod upon
neat's leather have gone upon my handiwork.*

1.1.22-26

ANSWER

Cassius sends Titinius to determine if the men near his tents are friend or foe. Before waiting for a
verified report, Cassius believes Pindarus' misreading of the situation and hastily commits suicide.

QUESTION

Who is asleep in Brutus' tent when he first sees the ghost of Caesar? (ANSWER ON PAGE 56)

LEPIDUS

THIRD OF THE NEW TRIUMVIRATE
"...a slight, unmeritable man"

Antony is unimpressed with Lepidus and, after sending him on an errand, tells Octavius so. Antony questions Octavius' choice of him as a potential world leader and says Lepidus will bear honors as an ass bears gold. Octavius gives Antony the freedom to do as he wishes, but defends Lepidus' military experience. Lepidus is not seen again in the play.

THE PLEBEIANS

COBBLER

Providing an element of clown-like humor early in the play, the cobbler is the quick-witted recipient of the tribunes' unjust harassment. With feigned innocence, the cobbler responds truthfully to each of the tribunes' questions, but with impish wordplay that sends them into fits of frustration. He is eventually sent home to consider at length his loyalties.

CARPENTER

His only line in the play is a response to the tribunes' question, "...what trade art thou?" The carpenter is likely amused to watch his companion, the cobbler, confound Flavius and Murellus with his clever wordplay. He is sent home with the others.

PLEBEIANS

Serving many roles, the plebeians are harassed by the tribunes at the beginning of the play, manipulated by Antony at Caesar's funeral and lied to by the triumvirate, who reduce their inheritance. At one point, the fickle plebeians wish to crown Brutus. They burn the conspirators' houses with brands from Caesar's funeral pyre and unjustly kill Cinna the Poet.

THUS DID MARK ANTONY

bid me fall down,
And, being prostrate, thus he bade me say:
Brutus is noble, wise, valiant, and honest.
Caesar was mighty, bold, royal, and loving.
Say I love Brutus, and I honor him.
Say I feared Caesar, honored him, and loved him.

3.1.128-133

ANSWER
Varro and Claudius are asleep in Brutus' tent when he first sees the ghost of Caesar.

QUESTION
Who kills Cinna the Poet after Antony's funeral oration? (ANSWER ON PAGE 59)

THE SERVANTS

LUCIUS AND STRATO
Brutus' faithful servants

Looking for a candle, Lucius finds Cassius' forged, which he gives to Brutus. Often seen dozing, Lucius functions as a counter to Brutus' stressful condition. Strato is Brutus' servant in battle. After several of the other servants refuse, Strato obeys Brutus' last request, holding his sword while Brutus runs on it.

SERVANTS OF CAESAR, ANTONY & OCTAVIUS
Servants of powerful men

Caesar's servant is sent to the priests who divine whether it is safe for him to travel on the ides of March. The servant brings word the priests found no heart in the sacrificial beast. Antony's servant delivers a request from his master for an audience with the assassins. Octavius' servant informs Antony of Octavius' whereabouts. Antony is touched when he expresses genuine grief over Caesar's body

PINDARUS
Bondservant of Cassius

Pindarus is sent by Cassius to the top of a hill to report on Titinius' mission. Based on what he witnesses from a distance, Pindarus gives an erroneous report that Titinius is captured. Cassius hastily orders Pindarus to stab him and he obeys. Afterward, Pindarus flees, now a free man.

DARDANIUS AND CLITUS
Brutus' armorbearer and his servant

With the battle lost, Brutus asks first Clitus, then Dardanius to kill him. They each refuse. The task is finally taken up by Strato, Brutus' friend and servant.

MESSENGER
Watchman for Antony and Octavius

A messenger—perhaps a watchman—arrives with the message that the enemy forces are approaching. He urges Antony and Octavius to respond immediately.

A QUICK REVIEW *of*

The Secondary Conspirators

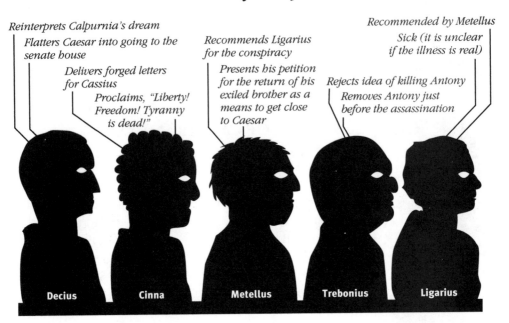

Reinterprets Calpurnia's dream

Flatters Caesar into going to the senate house

Delivers forged letters for Cassius

Proclaims, "Liberty! Freedom! Tyranny is dead!"

Recommends Ligarius for the conspiracy

Presents his petition for the return of his exiled brother as a means to get close to Caesar

Recommended by Metellus

Sick (it is unclear if the illness is real)

Rejects idea of killing Antony

Removes Antony just before the assassination

Decius **Cinna** **Metellus** **Trebonius** **Ligarius**

The Senators

The Tribunes

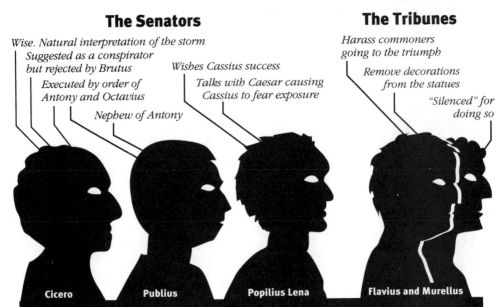

Wise. Natural interpretation of the storm

Suggested as a conspirator but rejected by Brutus

Executed by order of Antony and Octavius

Nephew of Antony

Wishes Cassius success

Talks with Caesar causing Cassius to fear exposure

Harass commoners going to the triumph

Remove decorations from the statues

"Silenced" for doing so

Cicero **Publius** **Popilius Lena** **Flavius and Murellus**

THE MINOR CHARACTERS

The Cautioners

"Beware the Ides of March"

Dismissed by Caesar as a dreamer

Warns Caesar one last time the day of the assassination

Writes a letter to Caesar naming all conspirators

Gives Caesar the letter, begging him to read it; Caesar puts the letter away to read later

The Poets

Mistaken for Cinna the conspirator

Brutalized by the mob for "bad verses"

Tries to stop Brutus and Cassius from arguing

Thrown out by Brutus

Soothsayer

Artemidorus

Cinna and another poet

The Allies

Impersonates Brutus when captured by Antony's troops

Discovered by Antony who treats him kindly

Provides news from Rome

Finds Cassius dead

Sent to find out if soldiers are allies or enemies

Kills himself when Cassius is found dead

Proclaims his name and patriotism in the field

Brother of Portia

Dies bravely in battle

Longtime friend of Brutus

Refuses to assist in Brutus' suicide

Lucilius and Messala

Titinius

Young Cato

Volumnius

ANSWER The plebeians kill Cinna the Poet after they are incited to riot by Antony's funeral oration. The killing marks the transformation of Rome from a republic (teetering on dictatorship) into a mobocracy.

A QUICK REVIEW *of*

The Soldiers

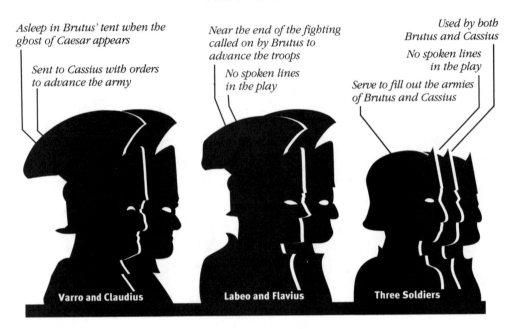

Asleep in Brutus' tent when the ghost of Caesar appears

Sent to Cassius with orders to advance the army

Varro and Claudius

Near the end of the fighting called on by Brutus to advance the troops

No spoken lines in the play

Labeo and Flavius

Used by both Brutus and Cassius

No spoken lines in the play

Serve to fill out the armies of Brutus and Cassius

Three Soldiers

The Servants

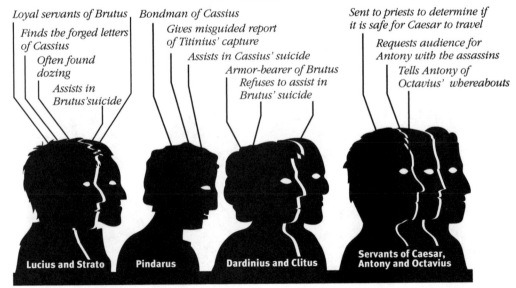

Loyal servants of Brutus

Finds the forged letters of Cassius

Often found dozing

Assists in Brutus' suicide

Lucius and Strato

Bondman of Cassius

Gives misguided report of Titinius' capture

Assists in Cassius' suicide

Armor-bearer of Brutus

Refuses to assist in Brutus' suicide

Pindarus

Dardinius and Clitus

Sent to priests to determine if it is safe for Caesar to travel

Requests audience for Antony with the assassins

Tells Antony of Octavius' whereabouts

Servants of Caesar, Antony and Octavius

THE MINOR CHARACTERS

The Soldiers

Capture Lucilius thinking he is Brutus

Inform Antony who quickly uncovers their error

Two Soldiers of Antony

Lepidus

Third of the new triumvirate of Antony and Octavius

Called "slight" and "unmeritable" by Antony

Lepidus

A Messenger

Informs Antony and Octavius that the enemy forces have arrived

Messenger

The Plebeians

Harassed by the tribunes Flavius and Murellus on their way to Caesar's triumph

Uses comic wordplay to frustrate his interrogators

Incited to riot by Antony's funeral oration

Kill Cinna the Poet without justification

Carpenter

Cobbler

People of Rome

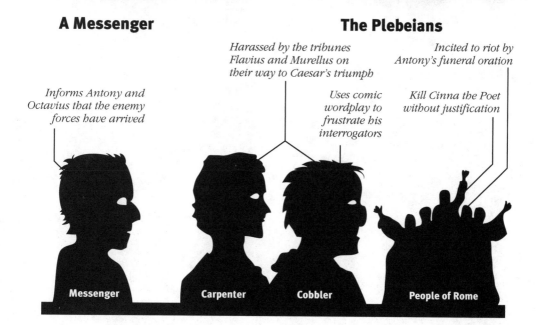

Plot
overview

The main plot of Julius Caesar *is straightforward; however, subtle complexities lie beneath the surface. Brutus' dilemma is an example of one such complexity—he is trapped in the rational-moral labyrinth of effecting a good through the exercise of an evil. Another complexity is the clash of world-views between the idealistic Brutus and his pragmatic brother-in-law, Cassius. A chief characteristic of the plot is the extended climactic transition from the assassination of Caesar to the spellbinding oration of Antony. Taken as a whole, the play will present the deliberately unresolved question: "Was the assassination of Caesar murder or tyrannicide?"*

The play is divided into thirds around Caesar's assassination.

FIRST THIRD: FORMATION OF THE CONSPIRACY

The first scene of the play shows Rome splintering into two factions: those who support Julius Caesar and those who are wary of his growing power. Cassius masterminds the formation of the second group into an assassination conspiracy, led by Brutus.

MIDDLE THIRD: ASSASSINATION/ORATION

On March 15, Caesar—thinking he will be crowned—is convinced to go to the senate, against several warnings to the contrary. There, in the first climax of the play, the conspirators kill him. Mark Antony, a close supporter of Caesar, is permitted by Brutus to speak at Caesar's funeral. In the second climax of the play, he cunningly turns the crowd against the conspirators, who flee for their lives to Greece.

FINAL THIRD: THE AFTERMATH—A POLITICAL VACUUM

Mark Antony and Octavius take control of Rome. Their armies meet with the armies of Brutus and Cassius at Philippi. Because of a mistaken communication after the first battle, Cassius commits suicide prematurely, leaving Brutus in a weakened position. After losing the second battle, Brutus commits suicide.

1. Formation of the conspiracy

Caesar's growing power is seen as a threat to the republic. using questionable methods, Cassius masterminds an assassination conspiracy, which is led by Brutus.

2. Assassination/oration

On March 15, Caesar is flattered into going to the senate—thinking he will be crowned—despite several warnings to the contrary. Once there, he is stabbed to death by the conspirators. Against Cassius' warnings, Brutus protects Antony from harm and allows him to speak at Caesar's funeral. In the second climax of the play, his careful, persuasive rhetoric turns the crowd against the conspirators. Brutus and Cassius flee to Greece.

3. The political vacuum

Octavius arrives in Rome. He and Antony take control of the army and treasury. On the plain at Philippi, their armies meet with the armies of Brutus and Cassius. The first battle is a draw, but Cassius commits suicide after mistakenly thinking they are overrun by the enemy. This leaves Brutus vulnerable. After being defeated in the second battle, Brutus commits suicide.

Acts 1 and 2	Act 3	Acts 4 and 5
Conspiracy	**Assassination**	**Aftermath**

Here is a graphic representation of these divisions.

THE CENTRAL ASSASSINATION

Note that the assassination of Caesar is in the exact center of the play. The climax of the play presents itself in two events. The first is the assassination, beginning with Caesar's warning-filled journey to the senate house and ending in his famous line, *"Et tu, Brute?* Then fall Caesar!"* ("You too, Brutus? Then fall Caesar!"). The second is Antony's funeral oration—a masterwork of persuasive rhetoric (If you are ever lucky enough to see this delivered by a seasoned Shakespearean actor, it is spellbinding). Think of the central extended climax presented in Act Three as being framed by the political jockeying in the first and final two acts.

The big question surrounding the assassination is this: *Was it tyrannicide or was it murder?* Brutus constructs the theoretical argument that it was tyrannicide. Antony presents the moving argument that it was murder. Shakespeare leaves the question deliberately unresolved.

The first third: the psychological knot of Brutus' dilemma.

CASSIUS LOBBIES TO ENLIST BRUTUS

At the Lupercalia races, Cassius approaches Brutus and gently leads him in the direction of conspiracy against Caesar. Though cautious, his tactics of flattery are clear, even to Brutus, who at one point asks, "Into what dangers would you lead me, Cassius…?" Cassius is satisfied with Brutus' admission that he is troubled by both Caesar's growing power and the subsequent vulnerability of the republic.

BRUTUS LEADS THE CONSPIRACY

Act Two opens a month later, with Brutus rationally constructing the case for Caesar's assassination (it is his greatest soliloquy). Brutus strains under the weight of his dilemma: Does a future threat to the republic justify a killing? Brutus' dubious intellective construct will haunt him throughout the play—near the end in the form of Caesar's ghost. Later in Act Two, the conspirators come to Brutus' house, treat him as the de facto leader and finalize the details of the assassination under his direction. Throughout the remainder of the play, Brutus' idealistic decisions will provide opportunities for Antony and Octavius to gain advantage.

1. Cassius lobbies to build an assassination conspiracy

After Caesar's growing power (demonstrated by his triumphant return to Rome) and his staged rejection of the crown at the Lupercalia, Cassius begins carefully lobbying his friends for a conspiracy to assassinate Caesar. His top priority is to convince Brutus to join the conspiracy, believing Brutus' noble reputation will lend much-needed integrity to their otherwise sordid undertaking.

2. Brutus' dilemma

Brutus wrestles with the dilemma: Is it right to murder Caesar to maintain the republic? Cassius complicates this moral dilemma with underhanded tactics (he delivers forged letters to Brutus from those praising his integrity and urging him to overthrow Caesar). The resulting predicament is by far the most interesting element of the play. After constructing a theoretical argument defending the assassination, Brutus agrees to lead the conspiracy.

Cassius lobbies   **Brutus joins**

Acts 1 and 2	Act 3	Acts 4 and 5
Conspiracy	**Assassination**	**Aftermath**

More detail shows the leadership moving from Cassius to Brutus.

BRUTUS AND THE TRAGIC IDEALISM

The movement from Act One to Act Two is shown by the movement from Cassius to Brutus as leader of the assassination conspiracy. Cassius recognizes that Brutus' noble reputation will provide the conspiracy with much-needed integrity. What he does not know, is that Brutus' high-minded idealism will prevent the conspirators from taking the necessary pragmatic steps to ensure their survival after the assassination. This high-minded idealism—the equivalent of a tragic flaw—will not plague either of their rivals, Antony or Octavius, in Acts Four and Five.

The second third: Caesar is assassinated and eulogized.

THE UNHEEDED WARNINGS

On the day of his assassination, Caesar is told not to go to the senate house by no fewer than four different people: his wife, his servant (bringing the message from the priests), the soothsayer and Artemidorus. By 3.1, Caesar has already ignored Calpurnia's pleas and the priests' advice, not to mention the soothsayer's early warning and the upheaval in the natural world. Now, on the way to the senate house, he will ignore the last of the consecution of warnings: the final warning by the soothsayer and Artemidorus' letter naming the conspirators.

After the assassination, the consequence of ignorance will switch to Brutus. Although warned by Cassius to kill Antony along with Caesar and cautioned by him not to provide Antony with an audience, Brutus believes the nobility of his own motives will be enough to restore peace. He cannot be more wrong. Antony, in the highlight speech of the play, shifts the fickle sympathies of the Roman public from the conspirators to Caesar. This shift of sympathies sets the countermovement into play, eventually leading to the tragic deaths of Cassius and Brutus.

1. The assassination: Caesar ignores the warnings

Caesar is afforded no fewer than six warnings not to go to the senate house: the upheaval in the natural world; the recommendation of the priests; the dream of Calpurnia; the two warnings of the soothsayer; and the letter of Artemidorus. On the way to the senate house, a complex Caesar is shown. He believes he will be crowned, but he is still benevolent enough to read his personal matter last (Artemidorus' letter). He stubbornly does not overturn his banishment ruling, but maintains he must be consistent to better serve Rome. Shakespeare crafts the moment into an unresolved question: Is this murder or tyrannicide? The play masterfully supports both conclusions.

2. The funeral oration: Brutus ignores the warning

Brutus' idealistic constructs will not allow him to heed the warning of Cassius not to permit Antony to speak at the funeral. Antony does indeed speak—one of the most moving speeches in all of Shakespeare's plays, certainly the greatest in *Julius Caesar*. Rome is transformed from a republic into a mobocracy, punctuated by the irrational murder of the poet, Cinna.

Cassius lobbies	Brutus joins	The Assassination	Funeral Oration

Acts 1 and 2	Act 3	Acts 4 and 5
Conspiracy	Assassination	Aftermath

The middle third is a strategic transition point in the play.

DOUBLE CLIMAX AND THE UNRESOLVED QUESTION

The double climax (or extended climax) of the assassination/oration events is the transition point from conspiracy to countermovement. At first glance, the aims of the conspirators seem to have been accomplished with the death of Julius Caesar. However, once Antony moves the Roman crowd to riot with his brilliant oration, the conspirators must flee for their lives. Instead of saving the republic, the conspiracy has unwittingly helped to fashion a mobocracy (the senseless murder of Cinna, the poet, is the representative event supporting this political degradation). So the question remains: *If Rome under Caesar was politically stable and reasonably governed, and Rome after his assassination is an anarchic mobocracy, then was the assassination murder or tyrannicide?* As with most of his larger concepts, Shakespeare astutely leaves the question unresolved.

The final third: the suicides of Cassius and Brutus.

THE CASCADE OF ERRORS

Brutus—after ignoring the advice of Cassius to neutralize Antony following the assassination by death or censure—makes another critical overruling: he plans to battle Antony and Octavius on the plains at Philippi. Arguments flare between Brutus and Cassius, but the two eventually reconcile. Against Cassius' better judgment, they lead their armies into battle. The first action is a draw: Brutus' army defeats Octavius' army, while Antony's army defeats Cassius' army. Cassius, seeing men near his tents and fearing the worst, asks Titinius to ride out to determine whether they be friend or enemy. As he does, Pindarus (Cassius' bondslave with better eyesight) misinterprets to Cassius what he sees, reporting that Titinius has been captured by the enemy (it's really Brutus' army crowding around him to celebrate their victory). Cassius commits a hasty suicide, leaving Brutus too weak to match armies against both Antony, a consummate soldier, and Octavius, a consummate politician. In the second action at Philippi, Brutus' army is routed and he commits suicide as his soldiers desert him.

1. The conspiracy strains under the demands of leadership

Antony and Octavius seize power and their bickering behind the scenes is shown. At Sardis, Brutus and Cassius confront one another in an argument stemming from their cross-philosophical outlooks. Cassius is a super-realist and has sold rank for much-needed military funding; Brutus is an intellective idealist and cannot allow transgressions for which they blamed Caesar to taint their own rule. The men find a means for understanding. Portia's suicide is discussed. The ghost of Caesar appears to Brutus, promising to appear again at Philippi.

2. The suicides of Cassius and Brutus; the rise of Octavius

The armies meet at Philippi (Cassius warns against this). The first battle is a draw—Brutus routs Octavius' wing, while Antony's wing overcomes Cassius. Through a miscommunication, Cassius believes the situation is hopeless and commits suicide, leaving Brutus vulnerable. In the second battle, Brutus is soundly defeated and he commits suicide to avoid capture. Octavius takes all of Brutus' loyal men into his own service.

Cassius lobbies	Brutus joins	The Assassination	Funeral Oration	Prelude to War	The Battles at Philippi
Acts 1 and 2		Act 3		Acts 4 and 5	
Conspiracy		Assassination		Aftermath	

The final details outline the end of the conspirators.

EMERGENCE OF THE TRIUMVIRATE

The aftermath of the assassination plots the downward trajectory of the conspirators and the forward movement of the emerging triumvirate. At Rome, Antony and Octavius fill the political vacuum created by the death of Julius Caesar, although they bicker over strategic details (Octavius is the winner). At Sardis, Brutus and Cassius do not bicker; they argue heatedly over idealistic points. Brutus comes out the winner, though his final strategy to meet the opposing armies at Philippi will be the last of his poor decisions. The political jockeying of the conspirators in Acts One and Two is now echoed by the political jockeying of the leadership on both sides. Caesar's ghost appears to Brutus in the final two acts, reminding him of the consequences he brought upon himself by leading the assassination. Brutus is not insensitive to the point. As he runs on his sword held by the reluctant Strato, he utters the words, "Caesar, now be still."

1.1 The triumphal return

Caesar is returning to Rome from his victory in the civil conflict against the sons of Pompey (historically, October, 45 B.C.). People await his triumphal parade, dressed in holiday clothing on a workday. Two tribunes exhort a group of craftsmen to return to work, since Caesar's victory is not over a foreign power, but fellow Romans. Afterward, the two tribunes strip the statues of any decorations and disperse any crowds, hoping to keep Caesar's growing popularity in check.

1.2 The Roman holiday

Juxtaposed by Shakespeare so closely to the triumphal return of Caesar as to purposefully seem on the same day, the Roman fertility holiday of Lupercalia was historically four months later on February 15. Caesar travels to the races with his entourage, including Antony, who will compete. A soothsayer warns Caesar to beware the Ides of March. During the race, Cassius cautiously attempts to win Brutus to the conspiracy in an extended conversation. After the race, Antony offers Caesar a crown, in a staged display to gauge the reaction of the crowd to his possible kingship. Caesar rejects the crown three times to the delight of the crowd. Frustrated by their reaction, Caesar offers the crowd his throat and then falls in an epileptic seizure. When he awakens, Caesar storms angrily from the stadium and confides his distrust of Cassius to Antony.

1.3 The storm

On what seems to be the night following the Lupercalia, Casca and Cicero take shelter together from a thunderstorm. Casca fearfully tells of the day's supernaturally-charged events: a slave's hand burned without injury; a lion at the Capitol glowered, but did not attack; an owl hooted in the marketplace during the day; men on fire walked the streets. Cicero takes a scientific stance. Before leaving, he offers that men interpret events to suit their own purposes. Cassius arrives and interprets the unnatural events to reflect the gods' attitude toward the unnatural state of Rome, which balances on the precipice of tyranny. He tests Casca's receptiveness to the conspiracy. Casca vows to go as far as any man. Cinna arrives. Cassius commissions him to deliver letters (his forged letters to Brutus) to specific sites where Brutus will find them.

Act One

1.3 The storm

1.2 The Lupercalia

1.1 Caesar's triumph

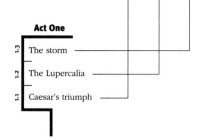

Cassius lobbies	Brutus joins	The Assassination	Funeral Oration	Prelude to War	The Battles at Philippi
Acts 1 and 2		**Act 3**		**Acts 4 and 5**	
Conspiracy		**Assassination**		**Aftermath**	

The opening events of the play are by far the most complicated.

1.1 CAESAR'S RETURN: A TENUOUS TRIUMPH

The tribunes try to prevent Caesar's return to Rome being marked by celebration. They represent the faction dissatisfied with the growing power and popular support Caesar is garnering. They will later be punished for this censorship.

1.2 THE LUPERCALIA: A POLITICAL CIRCUS

The juxtaposed fertility holiday (historically, four months after Caesar's return) includes some of the most complicated material in the entire play. The soothsayer warns Caesar to beware the Ides of March. Caesar, after thrice refusing the crown—by his own orchestration—offers his throat to the surprisingly delighted crowd and falls into an epileptic seizure (foreshadowing the assassination). During this political circus, Cassius attempts, with cautious flattery, to enlist Brutus' support of the conspiracy.

1.3 THE THUNDERSTORM: A MATTER OF PERSPECTIVE

The storm is interpreted in three ways: scientifically by Cicero, supernaturally by Casca and politically by Cassius. Cicero sums up the matter in what will become a thematic motif of the play: people interpret events to suit their own purposes.

2.1 Brutus assumes leadership

One month has passed. In the early morning hours of March 15, Brutus sits in his garden and constructs a theoretical argument for Caesar's assassination, namely, Caesar has the *potential* to cause harm to Rome. The conspirators arrive at his house: Cassius, Casca, Decius, Cinna (not the poet), Metellus and Trebonius. Because of his noble reputation, the conspirators treat Brutus as their leader and he assumes the role without protest. Placing idealism over pragmatism, he decides that they will leave Antony unharmed. They depart at three a.m. after agreeing to escort Caesar to the senate house at eight, later that morning. Portia enters and pleas for greater intimacy, sensing Brutus is troubled. Brutus delays the conversation, but agrees to tell her all later. She exits and Ligarius enters. Brutus enlists him to the conspiracy promising to divulge the details as they exit.

2.2 Calpurnia's protests

Caesar is warned not to go to the senate house by the unnatural events (a lioness gave birth in the street, graves opened, thunder roared, blood rained onto the capitol, ghosts shrieked), the priests (their sacrificial animal had no heart) and Calpurnia (she dreamed Caesar was a fountain, flowing blood for all Rome to bathe in). Decius arrives and flatters Caesar into going to the senate house (he tells Caesar he is to be crowned), reinterpreting the dream as a good omen. The other conspirators arrive at eight, along with Antony, and Caesar invites them to drink some wine with him before going to the senate house together.

2.3 Artemidorus' letter

Artemidorus purposes to hand Caesar a letter naming the conspirators, under the guise of handing him a petition on the way to the senate house. (Caesar will, of course, not read the letter when he gets it.)

2.3 Portia sends Lucius; the soothsayer's dread

It is nine a.m. and Portia—full of anxiety and foreboding—sends the servant, Lucius, to the senate house to observe Brutus and report back what he sees. The soothsayer passes them and they converse. He tells him he will speak to Caesar as he passes by, telling him that many unknown dangers are near. (Caesar will, of course, not listen to him when he does.)

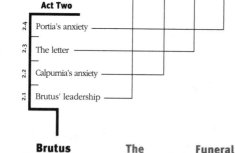

Act Two

2.4 Portia's anxiety
2.3 The letter
2.2 Calpurnia's anxiety
2.1 Brutus' leadership

1.1 1.2 1.3
Caesar's triumph
The Lupercalia
The storm

Cassius lobbies	Brutus joins	The Assassination	Funeral Oration	Prelude to War	The Battles at Philippi

Acts 1 and 2	Act 3	Acts 4 and 5

Conspiracy	Assassination	Aftermath

Anxiety and dread: the events on the morning of March 15.

2.1 MARCH 15, 3:00 A.M.

Brutus delivers his great soliloquy in which he intellectively constructs the argument for Caesar's assassination: a preemptive strike against a man who could possibly become harmful to the Roman republic. He leads the conspiracy in a meeting at his home, taking the reigns of authority from Cassius. Later, Portia's pleas for intimacy lend a humanizing character to the cold, political reality.

2.2 MARCH 15, 8:00 A.M.

Caesar is portrayed as vain enough to fall for Decius' flattery, but amiable enough to invite all the conspirators to wine before going to the senate house. Calpurnia's anxiety and her case against his traveling on the Ides of March falls on deaf ears.

2.3 and 2.4 MARCH 15, 9:00 A.M.

Artemidorus constructs a letter of warning (Caesar will fatefully delay reading it). Portia is beside herself with anxiety and cannot divulge her reason to Lucius for sending him to the senate house. The soothsayer positions himself for a final warning to Caesar as the leader passes by on the way to the senate house (the warning will, of course, be ignored).

3.1 Assassination of Caesar

On the way to the senate house, Caesar is warned by the soothsayer and Artemidorus. He ignores the former and delays reading the note from the latter. At the senate house, Popilius wishes Cassius' venture success and Cassius fears exposure. Trebonius lures Antony away as Metellus presents his petition for the return of his brother, whom Caesar has exiled. The other conspirators press in—as if to second the petition—and, as Caesar makes his case not to overturn the banishment, first Casca, then the others stab him with their daggers, killing him. The conspirators wash their hands in Caesar's blood and prepare to march through the streets, calling, "Peace, freedom and liberty!" Antony gains permission to approach and he shakes hands with each conspirator, pretending to befriend them. He appeals to Brutus' noble nature and secures his permission to speak at Caesar's funeral (against Cassius' warning) hoping to turn public opinion against the conspirators.

3.2 Antony's great oration

Cassius and Brutus each take a crowd and speak to them about their reasons for the assassination. Brutus nobly states that he had the highest interests of Rome in mind. The crowd tries to crown him, but he protests. Next, Antony speaks, bringing in the body of Caesar. In some of the greatest of Shakespeare's writing, he builds a subtle argument: the conspirators are all honorable men, but the legacy Caesar has left the people of Rome deserves outcry. He reads them the will of Caesar, detailing the money and public land he has left the citizenry. At last, he lifts Caesar's toga and shows them the horrible wounds. The crowd riots as Antony says smugly, "Mischief, thou art afoot!"

3.3 Cinna is murdered

The crowd rushes out to riot, burning the conspirators' houses with brands from Caesar's funeral pyre. Coming upon Cinna, the poet, the mob mistakes him for Cinna, the conspirator. When he tells them he is a poet, they reply, "Tear him for his bad verses!"

Act Three

3.3	The mob
3.2	The funeral
3.1	The assassination

1.1 Caesar's triumph
1.2 The Lupercalia
1.3 The storm
2.1 Brutus' leadership
2.2 Calpurnia's anxiety
2.3 The letter
2.4 Portia's anxiety

Cassius lobbies

Brutus joins

The Assassination

Funeral Oration

Prelude to War

The Battles at Philippi

Acts 1 and 2

Act 3

Acts 4 and 5

Conspiracy

Assassination

Aftermath

The conspiracy transforms into the countermovement.

3.1 ASSASSINATION: MURDER OR TYRANNICIDE?

The answer is left intentionally unresolved. Shakespeare portrays a Caesar cold enough to uphold a banishment, yet benevolent enough to delay reading Artemidorus' letter because he was told it concerns him personally. The stabbing is a bloody, claustrophobic moment foreshadowed by the epileptic seizure in 1.2.

1.2 FUNERAL ORATION: THE COUNTERMOVEMENT

The fickleness of the crowd is masterfully manipulated by Antony, a player at heart. Brutus, the theoretician, appeals to their logic. Antony, the reveler, appeals to their emotions. The end result is the transformation of a republic on the teetering edge of a benevolent dictatorship, into a mobocracy. With the chaos begins the countermovement against the conspirators.

1.3 RIOT: ROME WITHOUT RULE

The riot is unleashed by Antony, but could not exist without the actions of the conspirators. Rome, now without rule, is a violent anarchy where poets are murdered. The conspirators flee to Greece for their lives. Octavius and Antony—the political and military forces behind the emerging triumvirate, respectively—will capitalize on the ensuing political vacuum.

4.1 The triumvirs plot

At Antony's house, the emerging triumvirate—Antony, Octavius and Lepidus—write the names of those who will be executed as enemies of the state (historically, this proscription began in November, 43 B.C, some twenty months after Caesar's assassination). Lepidus' brother is listed, along with Publius, Antony's nephew. Lepidus is sent to Caesar's house to fetch the will. After he leaves, Antony denigrates him, saying they should soon expel him from the triumvirate. Octavius allows it, but defends Lepidus' military experience. Antony and Octavius agree to combine forces against Brutus and Cassius.

4.2 Brutus and Cassius meet

At Sardis, the two remaining conspirators, Brutus and Cassius, meet to discuss their differences. Cassius speaks to the point, saying Brutus has wronged him. Brutus tells him to lower his voice. He says they should discuss matters in his tent, rather than in front of the soldiers.

4.3 Argument and Reconciliation

The two conspirators argue. Brutus is outraged that Cassius would sell appointments to raise money and deny Brutus' request for funds. Cassius says he never denied Brutus money. The two argue heatedly, but eventually reconcile after Cassius hands his dagger to Brutus and asks him to kill him. A poet enters and the two generals share a joke at his expense before sending him away. Brutus and Cassius share a bowl of wine and Brutus says Portia has committed suicide by swallowing hot coals. Messala enters and tells them that the triumvirs have executed a hundred senators, including Cicero. Brutus, overruling Cassius, says they will fight Antony and Octavius at Philippi. That night, Caesar's ghost appears to Brutus, telling him they will meet again at Philippi.

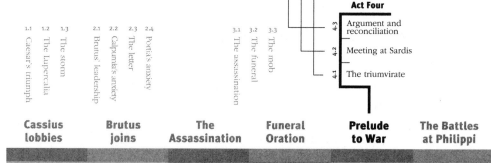

Act Four

4.3 Argument and reconciliation

4.2 Meeting at Sardis

4.1 The triumvirate

| 1.1 Caesar's triumph | 1.2 The Lupercalia | 1.3 The storm | 2.1 Brutus' leadership | 2.2 Calpurnia's anxiety | 2.3 The letter | 2.4 Portia's anxiety | 3.1 The assassination | 3.2 The funeral | 3.3 The mob |

| Cassius lobbies | Brutus joins | The Assassination | Funeral Oration | Prelude to War | The Battles at Philippi |

| Acts 1 and 2 | Act 3 | Acts 4 and 5 |

| Conspiracy | Assassination | Aftermath |

An intimate portrait of the two camps begins to emerge.

4.1 ROME: THE HEARTLESS TRIUMVIRS

Act Four opens with the triumvirs heartlessly conferring on which senators will be executed for their presumed involvement with the conspirators. Lepidus' brother and Antony's nephew, Publius, are both marked for death. The triumvirs are prepared to do anything to maintain power in Rome; the next scene will contrast this mindset with Brutus' stubbornness to uphold his ideals, even if it means death.

4.2 and 4.3 SARDIS: THE PASSIONATE CONSPIRATORS

Cassius' pragmatism is the perfect foil to Brutus' idealism. The two men passionately argue their two different worldviews in Sardis (ironically, Brutus claims rationalism over passion, but he is as passionate about his ideals as Cassius is about his own practicality). After they reconcile, Cassius learns over a bowl of wine that Brutus has been silently bearing the news of his wife's suicide. Perhaps because of this, he gives in to Brutus' decision to meet the enemy at Philippi. At the end of the scene, the ghost of Caesar appears to Brutus, puncturing the tenuous harmony. He cryptically identifies himself as "thy evil spirit, Brutus" and tells him they will meet again at Philippi.

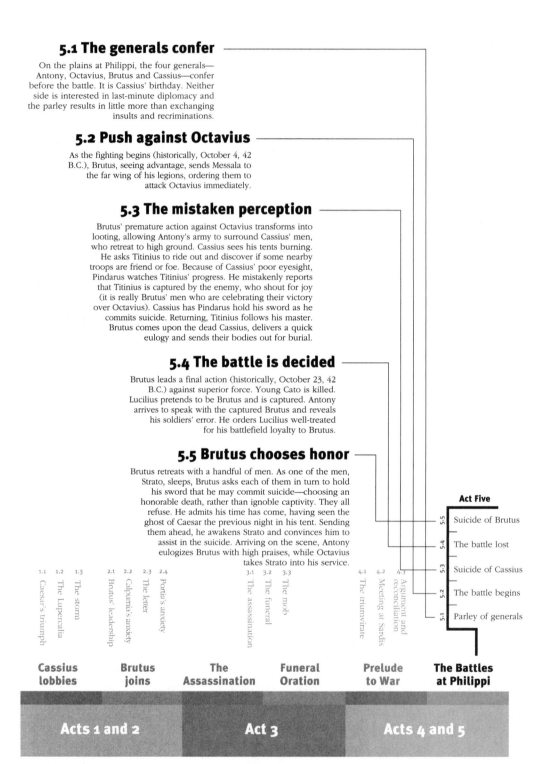

5.1 The generals confer

On the plains at Philippi, the four generals—Antony, Octavius, Brutus and Cassius—confer before the battle. It is Cassius' birthday. Neither side is interested in last-minute diplomacy and the parley results in little more than exchanging insults and recriminations.

5.2 Push against Octavius

As the fighting begins (historically, October 4, 42 B.C.), Brutus, seeing advantage, sends Messala to the far wing of his legions, ordering them to attack Octavius immediately.

5.3 The mistaken perception

Brutus' premature action against Octavius transforms into looting, allowing Antony's army to surround Cassius' men, who retreat to high ground. Cassius sees his tents burning. He asks Titinius to ride out and discover if some nearby troops are friend or foe. Because of Cassius' poor eyesight, Pindarus watches Titinius' progress. He mistakenly reports that Titinius is captured by the enemy, who shout for joy (it is really Brutus' men who are celebrating their victory over Octavius). Cassius has Pindarus hold his sword as he commits suicide. Returning, Titinius follows his master. Brutus comes upon the dead Cassius, delivers a quick eulogy and sends their bodies out for burial.

5.4 The battle is decided

Brutus leads a final action (historically, October 23, 42 B.C.) against superior force. Young Cato is killed. Lucilius pretends to be Brutus and is captured. Antony arrives to speak with the captured Brutus and reveals his soldiers' error. He orders Lucilius well-treated for his battlefield loyalty to Brutus.

5.5 Brutus chooses honor

Brutus retreats with a handful of men. As one of the men, Strato, sleeps, Brutus asks each of them in turn to hold his sword that he may commit suicide—choosing an honorable death, rather than ignoble captivity. They all refuse. He admits his time has come, having seen the ghost of Caesar the previous night in his tent. Sending them ahead, he awakens Strato and convinces him to assist in the suicide. Arriving on the scene, Antony eulogizes Brutus with high praises, while Octavius takes Strato into his service.

Act Five

5.5 Suicide of Brutus
5.4 The battle lost
5.3 Suicide of Cassius
5.2 The battle begins
5.1 Parley of generals

1.1 Caesar's triumph
1.2 The Lupercalia
1.3 The storm
2.1 Brutus' leadership
2.2 Calpurnia's anxiety
2.3 The letter
2.4 Portia's anxiety
3.1 The assassination
3.2 The funeral
3.3 The mob
4.1 The triumvirate
4.2 Meeting at Sardis
4.3 Argument and reconciliation

Cassius lobbies

Brutus joins

The Assassination

Funeral Oration

Prelude to War

The Battles at Philippi

Acts 1 and 2

Act 3

Acts 4 and 5

Conspiracy

Assassination

Aftermath

The defeat: Cassius and Brutus end their lives at Philippi.

CAESAR RESTS

The armies meet at Philippi in two decisive battles. In the first battle, Brutus appears to gain a quick victory over Octavius, but his men take to looting, giving Antony's legions opportunity to surround Cassius' army. In a thematic misinterpretation of reality, however, the pessimistic Cassius is quick to believe Pindarus' misguided report that the men near his burning tents are enemy soldiers. Impetuously, he commits suicide with the words, "Caesar, thou art revenged / Even with the sword that killed thee." Brutus, later surveying the scene, comments, "O Julius Caesar, thou art mighty yet! / Thy spirit walks abroad and turns our swords / In our own proper entrails." After the second battle against superior force, the retreating Brutus admits to his men that he knows his time is short, since the spirit of Caesar appeared to him the night before in his tent (we are not privy to their conversation). Finally, convincing Strato to assist in his suicide, Brutus dies with the soothing words, "Caesar, now be still; / I killed not thee with half so good a will."

Dilemma   **Extended Climax**   **Denouement**

| 1.1 | 1.2 | 1.3 | | 2.1 | 2.2 | 2.3 | 2.4 | | 3.1 | 3.2 | 3.3 | | 4.1 | 4.2 | 4.3 | | 5.1 | 5.2 | 5.3 | 5.4 | 5.5 |

1.1 Caesar's triumph
1.2 The Lupercalia
1.3 The storm

2.1 Brutus' leadership
2.2 Calpurnia's anxiety
2.3 The letter
2.4 Portia's anxiety

3.1 The assassination
3.2 The funeral
3.3 The mob

4.1 The triumvirate
4.2 Meeting at Sardis
4.3 Argument and reconciliation

5.1 Parley of generals
5.2 The battle begins
5.3 Suicide of Cassius
5.4 The battle lost
5.5 Suicide of Brutus

Cassius lobbies **Brutus joins** **The Assassination** **Funeral Oration** **Prelude to War** **The Battles at Philippi**

Acts 1 and 2   **Act 3**   **Acts 4 and 5**

Conspiracy   **Assassination**   **Aftermath**

The final timeline shows the dramatic flow of the plot.

FROM DILEMMA TO DENOUEMENT

The movement of the plot can now be seen from different levels of magnification. A sweeping view—from dilemma, through climax, to denouement—follows a similar path of conspiracy, through assassination, to its aftermath. On a ground level, the plot concerns are visible: Cassius lobbies to build the conspiracy, which Brutus eventually joins; the successful assassination appears midpoint in the play, proximal to the great funeral oration that begins the countermovement against the conspirators; the prelude to war is next, with its buildup of tension; finally, the battles at Philippi decide the outcome. Zooming in one more level, the scene details become apparent, beginning with Caesar's triumphant return to Rome and ending with the suicide of Brutus.

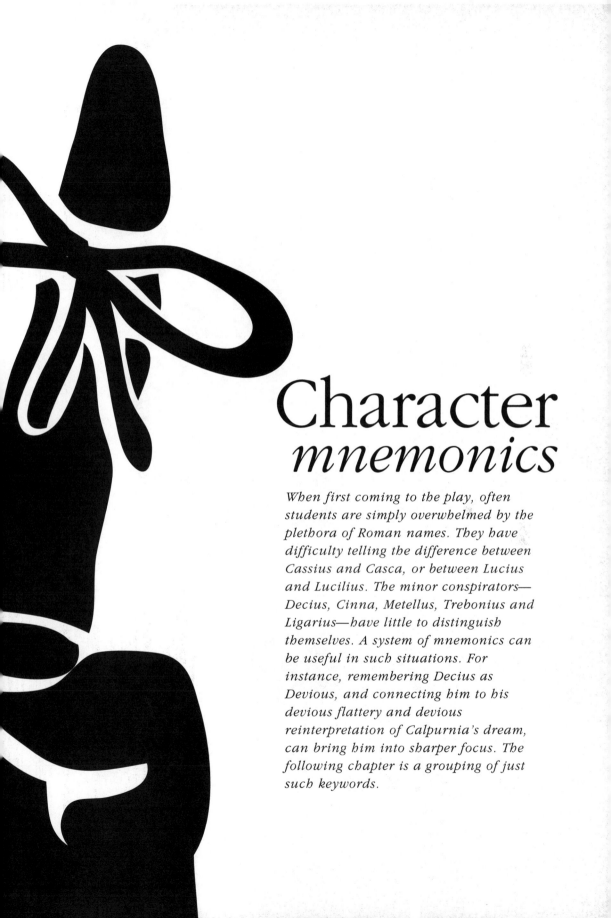

Character
mnemonics

*When first coming to the play, often
students are simply overwhelmed by the
plethora of Roman names. They have
difficulty telling the difference between
Cassius and Casca, or between Lucius
and Lucilius. The minor conspirators—
Decius, Cinna, Metellus, Trebonius and
Ligarius—have little to distinguish
themselves. A system of mnemonics can
be useful in such situations. For
instance, remembering Decius as
Devious, and connecting him to his
devious flattery and devious
reinterpretation of Calpurnia's dream,
can bring him into sharper focus. The
following chapter is a grouping of just
such keywords.*

Mnemonics: a way of remembering who is who in *Julius Caesar*.

THE PLETHORA OF *-us* names in Julius Caesar makes memorizing the characters a daunting task for the first-time playgoer or reader. However, through the use of suggestible keywords, it is possible to quickly learn the characters and one or two of their unique qualities. Take a few minutes to read through this chapter, quizzing yourself frequently. Whenever a visualization is suggested—for example, Trebonius blowing a trombone into Antony's ear, forcing him to leave the room—attempt to see the mental picture before going on. In this way, the characters will begin to sharpen their focus, leading to a better understanding of the play.

Brutus *Brutalized*	**Brutalized** by the necessity to kill Caesar to save the republic. **Brutalized** by the unforeseen consequences of the assassination.
Cassius *Cash*	Accused by Brutus of selling offices for **cash**. Accused by Brutus of valuing **cash** more than the noble ideals of the conspiracy.
Casca *Casket*	Wants to put Caesar into a **casket** himself when he sees him offer his throat to the crowd. Puts Caesar in a **casket** by being the first to stab the imperator.

Remember the major conspirators with three keywords.

USE THE THREE keywords—*brutalized, cash* and *casket*—to remember the architects of the conspiracy. Brutus, owing to his moral reflection, is brutalized by the thought of murdering Caesar. His great garden soliloquy in 2.1 shows him rationalizing his dilemma ("Can I further a good by committing an evil act?"), until he famously constructs—or invents—the reasons Caesar must die.

Cassius, on the other hand, is accused of a very tangible, almost pedestrian crime, reflecting his pragmatic disposition. To raise much needed cash for their military enterprise, Cassius sells offices. Brutus accuses Cassius of violating the very reason they killed Caesar: to maintain a system of rule based on ethics, respect and individual representation.

Casca, neither pragmatic nor intellectual, is the first to stab Caesar with his dagger (he does so in the back of the neck). Therefore, the term *casket* is appropriate to the initiator of the fatal stabbings.

Decius *Devious*	He is **devious** enough to convince Caesar to go to the senate house to be assassinated.
Cinna *Sinner*	He is a **sinner** because he delivers Cassius' forged letters to Brutus.
Metellus *Meddle*	He **meddles** with Caesar's decision to banish his brother.
Trebonius *Trombone*	Picture him blowing a **trombone** so loud Antony has to leave Caesar's presence before the assassination.
Ligarius *Ligament*	When he comes to Brutus' house, he is sick, so picture him sick with a torn **ligament.**

The five secondary conspirators require some visualization.

THE FIVE SECONDARY consiprators—Decius, Cinna, Metellus, Trebonius and Ligarius—are the most difficult of the minor characters to remember for people new to the play. Decius is perhaps the easiest to remember, in that his devious flattery and devious reinterpretation of Calpurnia's dream is the motivation for Caesar to leave the safety of his home. Trebonius can be memorable if the image of him blaring a trombone in Antony's ear until he leaves Caesar's presence can be recalled. In the same manner, a limping Ligarius, sick with a torn ligament and limping his way painfully to Brutus' house can be useful. Metellus and Cinna are more conceptual. Cinna (the conspirator, not the poet) sins against Brutus by placing Cassius' forged letters throughout the city. Metellus can be thought of a meddling in Caesar's affairs, when he calls Caesar's banishment of his brother into question.

Calpurnia *Calendar*	Calpurnia watches the **calendar** for the Ides of March and warns Caesar not to go out.
Portia *Pour*	Portia **pours** her heart out to Brutus in an attempt at intimacy. She later **pours** hot coals down her throat, committing suicide.

A famous warning and hot coals are used for the wives.

USE THE TWO keywords—*calendar* and *pour*—to remember the two wives in the play. Calpurnia, haunted by the soothsayer's warning, the supernatural events and her own terrifying dream, pleads with Caesar to stay at home on the Ides of March. Caesar relents momentarily, but is finally convinced by Decius, who reinterprets Calpurnia's dream to his own purposes, convincing Caesar it is safe to go to the senate house.

Portia is overcome with her husband Brutus' growing distance from her. In her entreaty for Brutus to take her into his confidence, she pours her heart out to him, even showing him a self-inflicted wound. Later in the play, we learn that, being so agitated and distressed over Brutus' long absence, she has died by pouring hot coals down her throat. The Stoic Brutus refuses to discuss it with his friends.

Antony *Antagonizes*	**Antagonizes** Brutus for the assassination of Caesar. **Antagonizes** the armies of Brutus and Cassius by defeating them.
Octavius *October*	Octavius' armies defeat those of Brutus and Cassius in the month of **October.**
Lepidus *Leper*	Antony is unimpressed with Lepidus as a triumvir and voices his concern to Octavius. Picture Antony treating Lepidus like a **leper.**

The keywords for the members of the new triumvirate.

THESE THREE KEYWORDS—*antagonize, October* and *leper*—help in remembering the men of the second triumvirate. Although they exchange few words prior to the assassination, Antony and Brutus each hold places in the close group surrounding Caesar. After the assassination, however, Antony antagonizes Brutus on the plains at Philippi on the eve of battle. Their argument grows so intense, they become anxious to take to the field.

Historically the two battles at Philippi took place in October, 42 B.C. Initially, Brutus was successful over Octavius. After Cassius' hasty suicide, Brutus' remaining army was overtaken by that of Octavius and Antony.

After sending Lepidus on an errand that a servant could perform, Antony refers to him as a "slight, unmeritable man." He complains to Octavius that Lepidus is not fit to be among the three who will inherit the Roman Empire. Octavius' laconic reply is not passionate in defending the third triumvir, as he points out Lepidus' merits as a soldier. Antony would prefer Lepidus be treated as a leper and plans to soon do away with him.

Cicero *Science*	Cicero justifies the unnatural storm by means of natural **science.** His scientific mind will not allow him to accept superstitious explanations.
Publius *Pub*	Antony's nephew, Publius, is marked for death during the proscription. Picture him in the **pub,** drowning his troubles in a pint of ale.
Popilius Lena *Pop*	Just as the entourage of conspirators enters the senate house behind Caesar, Popilius Lena **pops** up to wish Cassius good luck in his endeavor, then he **pops** over to speak to Caesar. His greeting makes Cassius fear their plot has been exposed.

Three unique senators: a scientist, a drinker and a jack-in-the-box.

THE NAMES OF the senators—Cicero, Publius and Popilius Lena—can be used to visualize their roles. Cicero is a scientist at heart. Viewing the pre-assassination storm as a natural weather phenomena, he cautions Casca that men will interpret events to suit their purposes (Cassius arrives to prove him right). Publius, the nephew of Mark Antony, is extremely distressed by the assassination, so much so that Brutus assures him no harm will come to him and Cassius directs him to go home. Later, he is proscribed by the triumvirs, a sign of how far they will go to gain control of Rome. He can be comically pictured in a pub, drinking his troubles away. The most active senator of the three, Popilius Lena can be seen popping from Cassius' side to Caesar's, wishing the former good luck with his endeavor and having an unheard conversation with the latter.

Lucilius *Silly us*	Impersonates Brutus on the battlefield. Picture the soldiers saying, **"Silly us** for believing you were Brutus!"**
Messala *Mess*	Comes upon the **mess** of the dead Cassius. Leaves to tell Brutus and returns to come upon the **mess** of the dead Titinius.
Titinius *Tie*	**Ties** the victory wreath around Cassius' head before following him in his suicide.
Young Cato *Cage*	Like an animal in a **cage,** Young Cato is surrounded by soldiers in the battle. He proclaims his name loudly for all to hear.
Volumnius *Volley*	**Volleys** back the request to assist Brutus in his suicide.

The allies all have keywords relating to events at Philippi.

THIS MNEMONIC GROUPING—*Silly us, mess, tie, cage* and *volley*—brings to mind the names of the allies of Brutus and Cassius. All the actions attached to their names occur at Philippi, as the conspiracy is coming to a close. Lucilius impersonates Brutus on the battlefield, trying to buy his friend more time to escape. After his capturing soldiers are made to look silly, Antony commends Lucilius' loyalty and orders him to be treated with kindness. Messala witnesses the aftermath of two suicides, those of Cassius and Titinius, truly a messy situation. Before following Cassius in death, Titinius completes his mission by tying the victory laurel given to him by Brutus around the head of his dead friend—a touching moment at the end of the play. After Brutus leaves the fighting, Young Cato takes up the task of spurring the troops on in battle. He is soon caged in like an animal, as he becomes surrounded by enemy troops. Before being killed, he proclaims his name loudly, "I am the son of Marcus Cato, ho! / A foe to tyrants, and my country's friend." As they are retreating, Brutus asks Volumnius to assist in his suicide, telling him the ghost of Caesar appeared to him twice. Volumnius declines, saying that it is no task for a friend.

Lucius *Loose*	Lucius holds a **loose** grip on his lute as he dozes off while playing for Brutus.
Pindarus *Pin*	Pindarus assists Cassius in his suicide when he **pins** his master with his own sword.
Strato *Straight*	Brutus is assisted in his suicide by Strato, who holds Brutus' sword **straight** for Brutus to run on it.

The servants' actions are the key to remembering them.

THREE MORE KEYWORDS—*loose, pin* and *straight*—make it easier to remember the names and actions of the servants. Brutus' servant Lucius is often sleepy in the play. As Brutus prepares for battle against Antony and Octavius, Lucius is called in to play the lute (it is very late at night). As he plays and sings, he falls asleep, loosening his hold on the instrument. During this time, Caesar's ghost appears to Brutus. Immediately after the ghost's departure, Lucius, in his sleep, comments that his strings have gone out of tune. He doesn't remember speaking when Brutus questions him about it.

From a hill, Pindarus misinterprets Titinius' encounter with allies. He tells Cassius that Titinius has been taken prisoner. Distraught over his loss of both the battle and a dear friend, Cassius, handing his sword to Pindarus, orders him to stab him. A bondsman to Cassius, Pindarus complies, pinning Cassius and ending his own bondage.

Seeing the battle lost and most of his army deserting, Brutus asks two of his servants and one friend, in turn, to assist him in his suicide. Each refuses. Brutus then sends his men ahead, save Strato. When he makes the request of Strato, the latter sadly complies, holding Brutus' hand and the sword straight.

Building
character

*A much overlooked aspect of
Shakespeare's* Julius Caesar *is the
masterful way in which the playwright
evokes character. Working within the
natural context of conspiracy and
subterfuge, Shakespeare brings forth
trait in sets of oppositional tensions:
the imperial Caesar is in physical
decline; the noble Brutus is
contemplating murder; the super-
realist Cassius is struggling against an
idealistic partner; the clever Antony is
moving a country with tactical
restraint. Amid the competing
motivations, personality begins to take
shape—often surprising the audience
with the complexity of its dimension.*

Expectation and the building of character through polarities

PERHAPS MORE THAN any other play, *Julius Caesar* presents the development of character, a process for dimensionalizing personality, through the use of behavioral polarities. Briefly stated, characters react against our expectations. Once a specific character's personality traits become entrenched in the mind of the audience, Shakespeare surrounds that character with a new set of circumstances, thereby exposing fresh, sometimes completely antithetical behavioral patterns than were seen before. Caesar, Brutus, Cassius, Casca, Antony—nearly all the major characters—move along a spectrum of seemingly contradictory behaviors throughout the course of the play. As a dramatist, Shakespeare masterfully navigates the difficult landscape between complicating or humanizing personality and destroying a character's credibility with the audience.

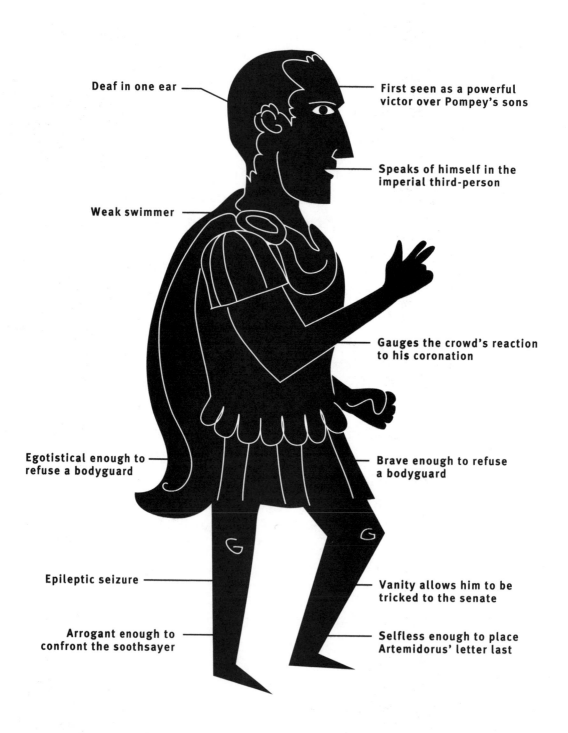

Deaf in one ear

First seen as a powerful victor over Pompey's sons

Speaks of himself in the imperial third-person

Weak swimmer

Gauges the crowd's reaction to his coronation

Egotistical enough to refuse a bodyguard

Brave enough to refuse a bodyguard

Epileptic seizure

Vanity allows him to be tricked to the senate

Arrogant enough to confront the soothsayer

Selfless enough to place Artemidorus' letter last

Caesar: power vs. vulnerability; ambition vs. selflessness

THE MAJESTIC CAESAR is developed most fairly between his polarities. Our first view of him is as a grand victor in the ceremonial journey to the Lupercal games. This view is immediately tempered by his wife's infertility *(Is she infertile or has Caesar grown impotent?)*, which serves the dual purpose of introducing a royal desire for an heir. After the games, Caesar's keen ambition is strategically thwarted by the crowd's surprisingly favorable response to his staged rejection of the crown. Moreover, no less than four physical infirmities are catalogued—Cassius' assertions that Caesar is both weak and sickly, the epileptic seizure and his own admission of hearing loss in one ear. This mix of power and vulnerability creates a three-dimensional man of far more interest than either a solely powerful or solely vulnerable dictator would. Caesar's final morning is another study in oppositions: he is at first intelligent enough to heed his wife's warnings, but vain enough to be tricked into thinking he will be crowned; he is arrogant enough to confront the soothsayer, but selfless enough to prioritize Artemidorus' letter last when he is told it touches him personally.

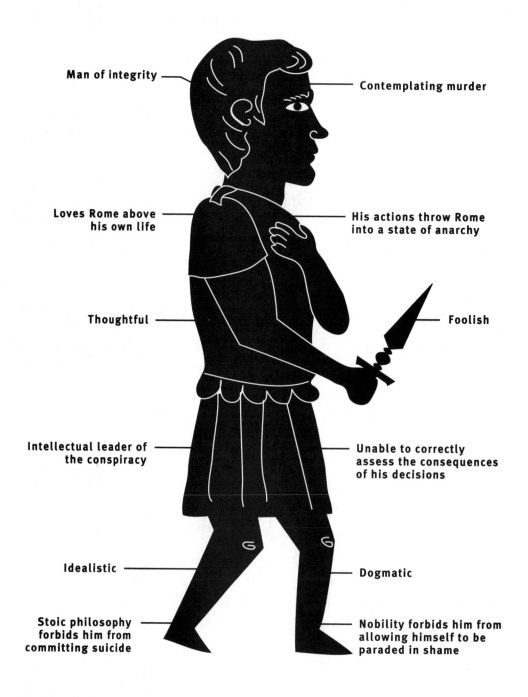

Man of integrity

Contemplating murder

Loves Rome above
his own life

His actions throw Rome
into a state of anarchy

Thoughtful

Foolish

Intellectual leader of
the conspiracy

Unable to correctly
assess the consequences
of his decisions

Idealistic

Dogmatic

Stoic philosophy
forbids him from
committing suicide

Nobility forbids him from
allowing himself to be
paraded in shame

Brutus: noble Roman vs. bloody conspirator; truth vs. perception

THE CONSUMMATE INTELLECTUAL prior to Hamlet, Brutus is overwrought with a sense of calamity at the growing power of Caesar. He is unable to entertain the pragmatic merits of a benevolent dictatorship under Julius Caesar and instead concentrates on the theoretical dangers of an oppressive despot. His motives are first questioned, however, during his all-important soliloquy in 2.1, when, alone in his garden, Brutus develops an intellective construct for the assassination—that is, he makes a theoretical, rather than a practical, case for murdering Caesar. This complexity of character (that of the noble conspirator) along with his dilemma (Should I perpetrate an evil, that good may come?) is the central concern of the play. In contrast to the gritty realism of Cassius, Brutus, by virtue or vice of his ponderous idealistic rationalism, must live in a psychologically invented realm. Although this unique quality recommends him as leader of the conspiracy, the consequences of his rational imagination bring about an unexpected cascade of foolish decisions: he doesn't question the veracity of the forged letters; he protects Antony from assassination; he provides Antony with a public forum; he rushes into battle at Philippi.

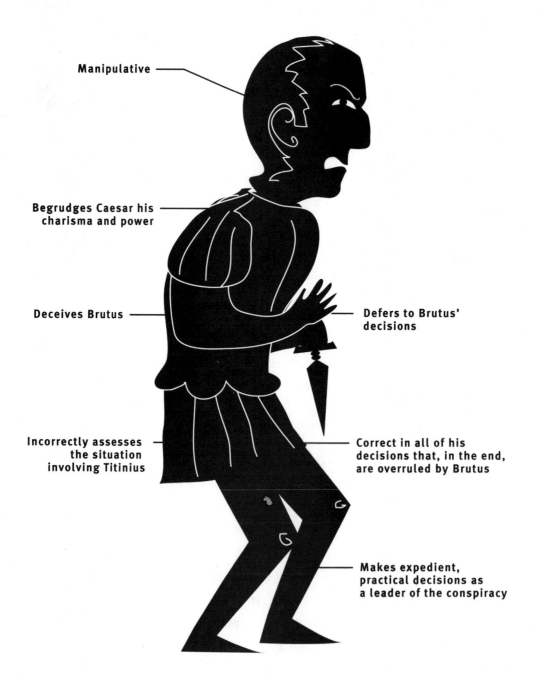

Manipulative

Begrudges Caesar his charisma and power

Deceives Brutus

Defers to Brutus' decisions

Incorrectly assesses the situation involving Titinius

Correct in all of his decisions that, in the end, are overruled by Brutus

Makes expedient, practical decisions as a leader of the conspiracy

Cassius: manipulative conspirator and the switch of sympathies

CASSIUS IS NOT the idealist Brutus is, but is instead motivated by his resentment of Caesar's charisma and power. He points out Caesar's infirmities and humanity with unrelenting energy. These qualities, instead of inspiring admiration in Cassius, serve to fuel his disdain. With no regard for ethical considerations, Cassius manipulates the naive Brutus, using first flattery and later deception in the form of a series of forged letters. Despite his lack of integrity, however, Cassius is correct in his recommendations (all of which Brutus overrules). Cassius, for example, supports Antony's assassination, strongly opposes providing him with a public forum at Caesar's funeral and disapproves rushing into battle against him at Philippi.

In Acts 4 and 5, Shakespeare surprisingly switches our sympathies for Cassius. In the final two acts, he is shown as a concerned friend of Brutus and as a realist who carries the added weight of his idealistic partner's noble, but foolish decisions. Brutus, for example, attacks Cassius for making expedient judgments (selling rank to raise much-needed money for the army) and afterward leads them both into a losing, winner-take-all battle. This empathy for Cassius culminates in his unnecessary suicide.

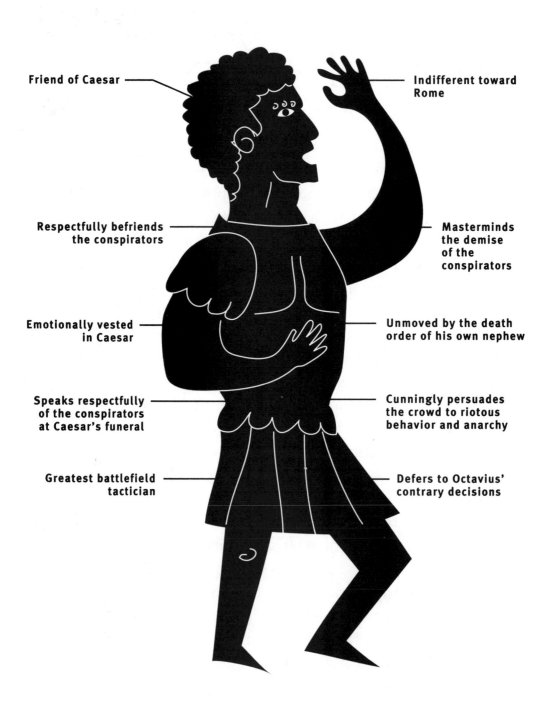

Friend of Caesar

Indifferent toward Rome

Respectfully befriends the conspirators

Masterminds the demise of the conspirators

Emotionally vested in Caesar

Unmoved by the death order of his own nephew

Speaks respectfully of the conspirators at Caesar's funeral

Cunningly persuades the crowd to riotous behavior and anarchy

Greatest battlefield tactician

Defers to Octavius' contrary decisions

Antony: Caesar's avenger or political opportunist?

ANTONY'S CHARACTER IS revealed not so much in surprising polarities as with cunning charades. He is first seen as a favorite of Caesar (who seems to admire Antony's athleticism and social reputation). The two share a sort of paternal relationship of understanding, essentially closer than the relationship Caesar and Brutus share, but perhaps lacking the depth. Caesar uses Antony in his obviously staged rejection of the crown and confides in Antony his suspicions about Cassius. After the assassination, Antony approaches the conspirators with great caution, thwarting expectations by shaking their bloody hands and requesting a private interview to hear their motivations.

Left alone, however, Antony reveals his actions to be a pretense. He skillfully steals the hearts of the Roman people and undermines some, if not most, of our sympathy for Brutus' circumstance. From the stirring of the mob until the end of the play, Antony becomes progressively colder—constructing the death list (which includes his nephew, Publius) and covertly lobbying to overturn Lepidus' status as triumvir. At play's end, the only personality as strong as Antony is Octavius.

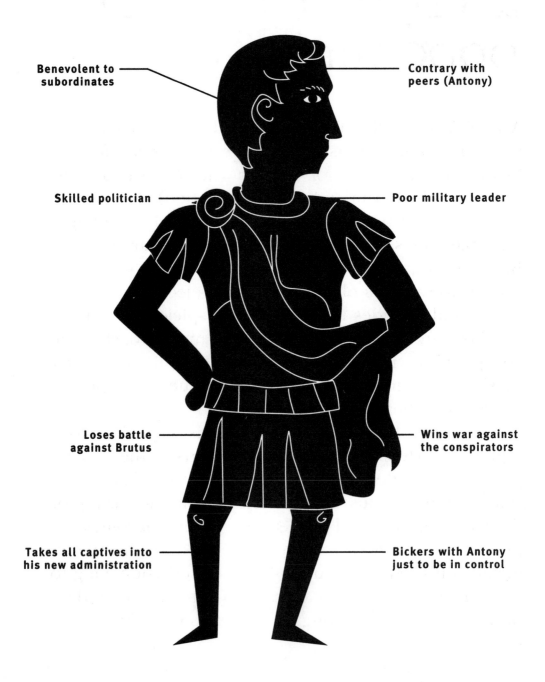

Benevolent to subordinates

Contrary with peers (Antony)

Skilled politician

Poor military leader

Loses battle against Brutus

Wins war against the conspirators

Takes all captives into his new administration

Bickers with Antony just to be in control

Octavius: egotistical contrarian vs. benevolent heir

OCTAVIUS ENTERS the play after the climactic assassination and oration scenes. His is certainly a smaller part among the major characters. It is as if he has no work to do—Antony has already marshaled the countermovement against the conspirators—yet historically we know he will have all the work of building Rome. Shakespeare portrays Octavius as an "untouchable," seeming to rise above the mundane landscape the other characters act upon. When he does interact with Antony (our first view of him), he is a deliberate contrarian: placing Lepidus' brother and Antony's nephew on the death list; laconically defending Lepidus from Antony's verbal attack; and choosing the right wing for his own army contrary to Antony's suggestion. To balance this triviality, Shakespeare shows the victorious Octavius, as a benevolent heir of the mighty Caesar, taking all captives into his service. This behavior is perfectly motivated—Octavius, a skilled political strategist, struggles only against his equals (in this case Antony), while cementing a loyal base of support for his new administration.

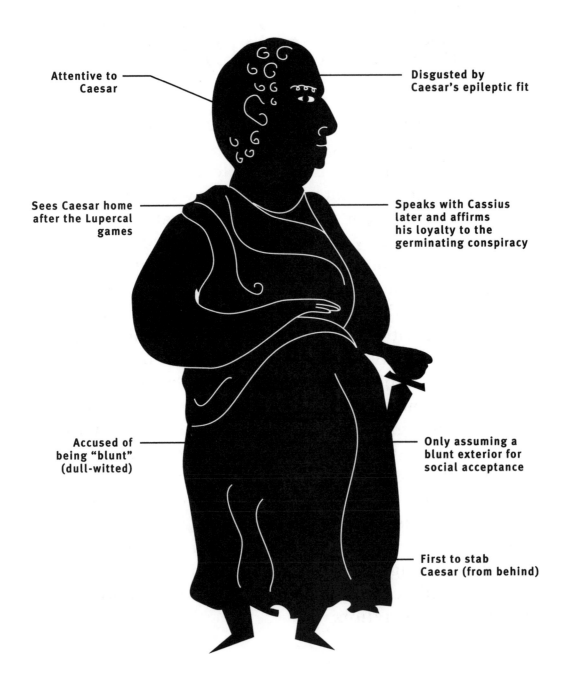

Attentive to Caesar

Disgusted by Caesar's epileptic fit

Sees Caesar home after the Lupercal games

Speaks with Cassius later and affirms his loyalty to the germinating conspiracy

Accused of being "blunt" (dull-witted)

Only assuming a blunt exterior for social acceptance

First to stab Caesar (from behind)

Casca: loyal member of the entourage vs. backstabbing plotter

AS A MEMBER of Caesar's entourage, Casca first appears to be overly responsive to Caesar's needs. He stops the entourage on the way to the Lupercal games, for instance, to bring full attention to Caesar's call for Calpurnia. Being close to Caesar—physically, not devotionally—he is able to repeat the details of the crown rejection and the subsequent epileptic seizure with little effort. During the irreverent telling of the story, however, the true Casca emerges, with loyalties ostensibly to Caesar, but in reality only to himself. After Casca leaves, Brutus calls him "a blunt fellow" (meaning a dull-witted fellow), but Cassius defends him, saying it is an act, assumed for social acceptance. It is this counterfeit persona that defines Casca for the remainder of his appearances (he is not seen in the final two acts). Testing him, Cassius calls into question Casca's loyalties to the germinating conspiracy. Casca responds that he will go as far as any man to correct the wrongs in Rome. And so he does. Casca is the first to stab Caesar—in Plutarch's version as in Shakespeare's—appropriately plunging the dagger in from behind and uttering the line, "Speak, hands, for me!"

Scene
by scene

*This chapter serves as a summary of the
action and dialogue in each scene of
the play. The scene breaks in
Shakespeare's plays are arbitrary—they
were not noted in the original
documents—but, except in rare
instances, they occur when the stage
completely clears.* Julius Caesar
*contains several short scenes (especially
in Act Five). These, therefore, have been
combined onto a single summary page,
as with 5.2 and 5.3, among others.
Especially long scenes, such as 2.1 and
3.1, were broken into two summaries.
We recommend you read this chapter in
one or two sittings, if time allows,
thereby gaining a large, sweeping view
of* Julius Caesar *before tackling the
actual text of the play.*

ACT 1, SCENE 1

The tribunes accost craftsmen who are on their way to Caesar's triumph.

THE TRIBUNES FLAVIUS and Marullus—officials elected to protect the rights of citizens—approach a group of craftsmen dressed in holiday clothes. Flavius tells them to go home, saying they should be dressed in work clothes, since it is a workday. Flavius demands one of the craftsman state his occupation. The man answers plainly that he is a carpenter. Marullus says that he should then be dressed in his apron and carrying his ruler.

Marullus asks another of the craftsmen to state his occupation. The tradesman responds obliquely that the tribune would consider him a cobbler. Marullus demands he answer more directly. In the first of a series of puns, the tradesman plays on the central idea that he can mend bad soles (souls) and can therefore be of service to Marullus. At last Flavius interrupts, clarifying that the tradesman is, in fact, a cobbler. He asks the cobbler why he is leading the others through the streets, rather than working. The cobbler jokes that he is trying to wear out the shoes of his companions as they make their way to Caesar's triumphal procession.

Marullus asks angrily why the tradesman are celebrating the return of Caesar to Rome, since Caesar is returning empty-handed from an internal civil dispute over the sons of Pompey, rather than with hostages and spoils from a foreign war.

Marullus reminds the citizens that not too long ago they clamored up walls and rooftops, waiting patiently to cheer the passing chariot of Pompey. He scolds them now for their vacillating affections, aghast that they would leave work to don their holiday clothes and throw flowers for the vanquisher of Pompey's sons. He recommends they return home, fall on their knees and pray the gods remove the pestilence that must be surely be coming to Rome because of their ingratitude.

Flavius joins in, telling them to weep into the Tiber river until its banks overflow. As the citizens disburse, he points out to Marullus how the people, in their shame, have no response to the accusations.

Flavius then directs Marullus to go toward the Capitol and remove any decorations from the statues, while he takes a different route and does the same. Marullus questions the wisdom of doing this during the Feast of Lupercal. Flavius remains firm, repeating the directive and adding they should both disburse any crowds they encounter on their way. He says that in doing this, they will prevent Caesar from thinking too highly of himself and behaving like a dictator.

DISPARITY
In October, Caesar returned to Rome in triumph over the sons of Pompey. The Feast of Lupercal—celebrating the mythological founding of Rome by Romulus and Remus—took place in February. Shakespeare removes the four-month disparity between these two events, placing Caesar's triumphal procession at the time of the Lupercal.

ACT 1, SCENE 2

A public warning; the refusal of the crown; the beginnings of conspiracy.

ON THE FEAST of the Lupercal, Caesar and his entourage travel in ceremonial pomp to the festival race, where Antony will compete. Caesar directs his wife, Calpurnia, to stand where Antony can touch her during the race, placing hope in the widely held superstition that doing so will cure her infertility. A man calls out to Caesar and Caesar stops the procession, bidding him to step forward. It is a soothsayer who warns, "Beware the Ides [the 15th] of March."

Caesar calls the man a dreamer and then continues to the race, with Cassius and Brutus staying behind. Cassius points out Brutus' growing aloofness, but Brutus says the source is simply his own internal conflict. Cassius then alternately praises Brutus' reputation, while denigrating Caesar's, increasing the intensity of his argument as the conversation progresses. Brutus, skeptical at first, soon voices his own discontent over Caesar's burgeoning power. Cassius tells a story that Caesar was drowning and needed to be saved by Cassius when they were both young men. Twice the conversation is interrupted by loud cheers from the crowd.

Cassius comes to the point of his argument: Caesar, a mere man, inferior in many respects to them both—especially to Brutus—has become a dangerously powerful political figure in Rome. Brutus agrees to speak further about these matters at another time. He closes with the assertion that he would rather live as a common peasant than be a Roman citizen in the oppressive regime that is currently developing under Caesar.

The games finish and Caesar returns with his entourage. Brutus points out that Caesar looks angry. Cassius says they will ask Casca to tell them what happened. Caesar privately calls Antony to his side. He tells Antony that, if it were possible for Caesar to fear men, then he would fear men like Casca: lean, unsmiling and discontented.

Everyone exits but Casca, Cassius and Brutus. Casca recounts that after the race, Antony offered his victory laurel wreath three times to Caesar (obviously this had been arranged in advance to gauge the crowd's reaction); each time Caesar refused the crown, causing the crowd to cheer. The third time, Caesar became overwhelmed by the frustration of the crowd cheering his ceremonial refusal of the kingship. He offered his throat to be cut and fell into an epileptic seizure. Casca agrees to sup at Cassius' house the next day and exits. Brutus agrees to meet with Cassius as well and he, too, exits. Alone, Cassius says he will enlist Brutus to his cause. He plans to provide Brutus with forged letters praising Brutus' reputation and alluding to the dangers of Caesar's growing ambitions.

FORESHADOWING
Casca's description of the seizure at the Lupercal games foreshadows elements of the assassination. For example, Caesar's throat offering to the crowd evokes the eight-person stabbing. Also, the choking breath of the multitude calls to mind the encircling of the conspirators. Finally, similar language is used to describe both moments: *"And so he fell"* and *"Then fall, Caesar"*.

ACT 1, SCENE 3

The thunderstorm; Cassius furthers the conspiracy; the forged letters.

TOGETHER, CICERO AND CASCA take shelter from a thunderstorm. Commenting on the lightning and earth-rattling thunder, Casca asks Cicero how he can remain calm when the gods must be either embroiled in civil war or incensed at some human offense. He relates strange, unexplainable sights he's seen: a slave's hand burst into flame without being scorched; a lion he encountered at the Capitol passed by without attacking; owls hooted during the day in the marketplace.

Cicero's answer is pithy and will become a major theme for the play: men interpret events to suit their own purposes. After confirming Caesar will be at the Capitol the next day, Cicero bids Casca good-night. As he leaves, Cassius arrives and takes shelter with Casca. He boasts about strolling through the storm, offering his bared chest to the lightning. Shocked, Casca questions the wisdom of tempting the gods. Cassius scoffs and says the gods are indicating their displeasure at the unnatural condition of Rome, which allows a mere man to storm about and roar like a lion in the Capitol. When Casca asks if he means Caesar, Cassius' response is purposely ambiguous.

Casca informs Cassius that the following day the senate intends to make Caesar king over their foreign possessions. Upon hearing this, Cassius declares that he will free himself from slavery by suicide. He complains that Caesar would not have so much power if the Romans did not allow it. In a move calculated to test Casca's sympathies, Cassius stops himself, saying that perhaps Casca is a willing subject and will take offense at him speaking out in this way. Casca replies that he is not a tattle-tale and he offers Cassius his hand, saying he will go as far as anyone else in a plan to put right these terrible injustices.

Satisfied, Cassius takes Casca's hand and tells him certain noble Romans wait for him at the portico of Pompey's theater to discuss a dangerous but worthy plan. Cinna approaches and Casca advises caution. Cassius identifies him, however, and greets Cinna as a friend of the undertaking. Cinna expresses his desire for Cassius to win Brutus to their cause. Cassius tells him not to be concerned, but to deliver some letters to specific locations—the magistrate's chair, Brutus' window and Old Brutus' statue—where Brutus is certain to find them. He then tells Cinna they will meet at Pompey's theater.

When Cinna departs, Cassius tells Casca they will meet with Brutus before morning to convince him to join them. Casca points out that Brutus is so highly regarded, he will lend credibility to their cause.

STORM
It is a typical device of Shakespeare to show nature rebelling against the death of a king or a great leader. Renaissance folklore integrally tied regicide with a backlash of unnatural occurrences.

ACT 2, SCENE 1 PART 1

Brutus' case for assassination; he meets with the conspirators.

A FEW HOURS before sunrise, Brutus walks in his garden. He is unable to discern the time and calls to his servant Lucius to light a candle in his study. Alone, Brutus develops a case for the assassination of Caesar. Although he admits Caesar has done nothing wrong, he argues that crowning a man imbues him with dangerous power. Caesar, he believes, may abuse his power at Rome's expense. He constructs a closing metaphor: Caesar is a serpent's egg that must be killed before it hatches.

Lucius returns with a sealed letter he found at Brutus' study window. Brutus takes the letter and asks Lucius to confirm that it is truly the Ides of March. With Lucius gone, Brutus reads the letter. It is one of Cassius' forgeries and it contains a cryptic message, calling Brutus to action. Brutus muses that he found other letters like this one containing the same coded line: "Shall Rome, etc." Brutus interprets the line to his own purpose: "Shall Rome stand under one man's awe?" Lucius comes back and informs Brutus that it is, indeed, the Ides of March. They hear knocking at the gate and Lucius is sent to answer it.

Left alone, Brutus comments that he has not slept since Cassius first incited him against Caesar. Revealing the substance of his thoughts, he draws a parallel between his conflicted psychological struggle and a political insurrection.

Lucius returns, saying Cassius waits at the door, along with several men who hide behind their hats and cloaks. Knowing them to be the conspirators, Brutus has Lucius show them in. Cassius introduces the men to Brutus, who welcomes them each in turn: Trebonius, Decius, Casca, Cinna and Metellus Cimber. Cassius draws Brutus aside for a private conversation.

Shakespeare has the remaining conspirators dispute a minor point— namely, *which direction is east?* The group cannot reach consensus over this trivial question, causing the audience to wonder at their chances of success in assassinating the most powerful man in Rome.

Cassius and Brutus rejoin the others. Cassius suggests they all swear a vow of their commitment. Brutus counters that no oath should be sworn, since their suffering under the tyranny of Caesar should be sufficient motive. The cause they have undertaken, he believes, is intrinsically motivating. He continues, saying Romans such as they require no oaths. Cassius, Casca, Cinna and Metellus recommend enlisting Cicero. Brutus again counters the group's suggestion, arguing that Cicero will never follow after what others have begun.

IDES
The original Roman calendar appeared around the 7th century B.C. and consisted of 304 days over 10 months beginning with March. The days of the month were determined by counting backward from three dates: the calends (first of the month), the ides (middle of the month, falling on either the 13th or the 15th), and the nones (9th day before the ides).

ACT 2, SCENE 1 PART 2

The conspirators' meeting concludes; Portia pleads for Brutus' confidence.

AS THE MEETING CONTINUES, Decius asks if any others need to be sacrificed along with Caesar. Cassius suggests that since Antony and Caesar are so close, Antony should be killed as well. He reasons further that if Antony uses his resources, he will be able to harm the conspirators after the assassination. Brutus disagrees, saying Antony's death will make them appear too violent, as though they were killing Caesar out of hatefulness and Antony out of jealousy.

Brutus then speaks of the conspirators' case against Caesar's ambition. He regrets they cannot separate the spirit from the man and thereby destroy Caesar's ambition, rather than Caesar himself. Brutus describes the proper attitude when killing Caesar as boldness, instead of anger—urging them to display reverence, as though presenting a sacrifice to the gods, rather than a meal for dogs. He instructs them to only let enough anger stir in them to do the deed and afterward to feel remorse. Then, he maintains, they will appear as ones righting a wrong, rather than as murderers. He concludes, saying Antony will not be a threat to them once Caesar is dead.

Cassius says he still fears Antony because of his love for Caesar. Brutus tells Cassius not to think of Antony. Trebonius agrees with Brutus, and he predicts Antony will surely laugh with them later.

The clock strikes three. Cassius, knowing they must finish their business, points out they do not know for sure if Caesar will venture outside because of his growing superstition. Decius assures them that he will persuade Caesar. Cassius says they will go to Caesar's house at eight o'clock to escort him. Metellus recommends Ligarius to their conspiracy, saying he was publicly berated by Caesar for speaking well of Pompey. Brutus tells Metellus to send Ligarius to him and he will enlist Ligarius to their cause. The conspirators part as Brutus urges them to assume pleasant faces and bear their cause as Roman actors.

Alone, Brutus calls for Lucius and quickly realizes he is fast asleep. Portia comes outside and reminds Brutus of his changed behavior, saying he has grown increasingly distant and unkind to her. Brutus replies that he is merely not feeling well. Portia is unbelieving and she pleads on her knees to be taken into his confidence. She tells him of a wound she has inflicted in her thigh to prove her ability to keep secrets. Brutus begs the gods to make him worthy of his noble wife. He says he will tell all to her soon. A knock interrupts them. It is the sickly Ligarius. He tells Brutus that he will be well if Brutus leads him in a worthy cause. They depart for Caesar's house.

DISAGREEMENT
Several times in the play, Cassius is seen advising against Brutus' decisions. He disagrees with the directive not to kill Antony, he is against allowing Antony to speak at Caesar's funeral, and finally he advises they wait for Antony and Octavius' armies rather than advance to meet them at Philippi.

ACT 2, SCENE 2

Calpurnia's dream; Caesar resolves to go to the senate house.

LATER THAT MORNING, Caesar is at home in his nightclothes. Alone, he comments that neither heaven nor earth were peaceful the night before. He says that even Calpurnia cried out three times in her sleep, "Help, ho! They murder Caesar!" A servant enters. Caesar orders him go to the priests and request a sacrifice to determine his fortune. As the servant exits, Calpurnia comes forth and tells Caesar that he will not leave the house.

Caesar counters, saying when his enemies see his face, they will vanish in fear. At this, Calpurnia tells him reports of strange happenings seen by the night watch: a lioness giving birth in the street, graves opening and giving up the dead, soldiers of fire making war in the clouds until it rained blood on the Capitol, ghosts shrieking. Her husband remains firm, saying the signs are as much for everyone else in the world as they are for him. Calpurnia disagrees, arguing that the natural order of the world is not upset by the death of beggars. Caesar answers with the famous lines, "Cowards die many times before their deaths / The valiant never taste of death but once."

He goes on to express how strange he finds it that men fear death, since it is an inevitability that will come in its appointed time. The servant returns from the priests with news that the sacrificial beast had no heart. Caesar interprets this to mean the gods are testing his courage and states again that he will not stay home. Calpurnia drops to her knees, begging her husband to stay. Caesar is moved by her show of emotion and he relents, saying he will stay for Calpurnia's sake.

Decius arrives to escort Caesar to the senate house. Caesar informs him that he will not go, stating pointedly that it is not because he cannot, nor that he dare not, but that he will not. Decius asks him for an excuse to give to the senators, but Caesar says that his will to not go is the only excuse necessary. He privately confesses to Decius, however, that Calpurnia dreamed Caesar's statue flowed with 100 spouts of blood and many Romans washed their hands in it. Decius cleverly reinterprets the dream, saying it means that Caesar will nourish Rome. He continues that the senate has decided to crown Caesar that day and suggests that jokes will be made if Caesar stays home. Excited, Caesar calls for his robe.

It is now eight o'clock and the other seven conspirators arrive to Caesar's warm, ebullient greetings. Antony also arrives and Caesar jokes that he is up early from his night's revelry. In high spirits, he invites them all to share some wine with him before leaving together for the senate.

HUNDRED
In Calpurnia's dream, Caesar's statue poured forth one hundred spouts of blood. We later find that one hundred senators were killed under suspicion of involvement in the conspiracy—a spout of blood for each senator.

ACT 2, SCENES 3 & 4

Artemidorus' letter of warning; Portia sends Lucius to the senate.

ARTEMIDORUS, A TEACHER of rhetoric, reads a letter he has written to Caesar. In the letter, he carefully names each of the eight conspirators, beginning with Brutus. With every name, Artemidorus attaches a special warning: beware of Brutus; pay attention to Cassius; stay away from Casca; watch out for Cinna; do not trust Trebonius; take notice of Metellus; Decius does not love you; Ligarius has been wronged by you.

The letter continues, saying all of these men have the same thought, directed against Caesar. He concludes with a warning that if Caesar is not immortal, then he should be heedful—a false sense of security will lead to ensnarement. Ending the letter with a prayer, he signs it, "Thy lover, Artemidorus." In soliloquy, he vows to stand in a strategic place as Caesar passes on his way to the senate house. He says he will present the letter as though it were a formal petition for Caesar. He grieves that someone as virtuous as Caesar has to suffer the envy of other men. As though speaking to Caesar, he pleads with him to read the letter.

The next scene opens with Portia ordering Lucius to the senate house. Immediately after giving the order, she impatiently asks him why he has not gone yet. Lucius responds that Portia has not told him the purpose for his errand. Portia replies irrationally that he could be there and back by the time she tells him what she wants. Portia thinks aloud, urging herself to be steadfast and not speak what is in her heart. She says that she has the mind of a man, but the strength of a woman and admits it is difficult for a woman to keep secrets.

Seeing Lucius waiting, she scolds him for still being there. Lucius, his own patience tried, asks her if he should simply run to the senate house and then return. Portia surprisingly agrees, telling Lucius to return and tell her if

Brutus is well. She instructs him to mind what Caesar does and who stands near him. Finishing, she hears a clamor, and says it is sounds like a fight brought on the wind from the Capitol.

At nine o'clock, the soothsayer passes by and Portia stops him to ask if Caesar has gone yet to the senate. The soothsayer replies that he has not. He says he plans to stand and plead with Caesar to think about himself. Portia asks if the soothsayer knows of any harm intended toward Caesar. The soothsayer tells her he knows no harm of which he is sure, but much that he fears. He departs, looking for a place to speak to Caesar. Portia quietly prays for Brutus' success, but stops herself, seeing Lucius. She urges him to run and tell Brutus that she is happy. They part ways in opposite directions.

SECRETS
Portia's ability to keep Brutus' secret changes between 2.1 and 2.4. When we first see her, she has wounded herself in her earnestness for his confidence, assuring him she will not disclose his counsels. Here in 2.4, she says how hard it is to keep secrets, even inadvertently beginning to blurt Brutus' secret to Lucius before stopping herself.

ACT 3, SCENE 1 PART 1

The final warnings are given; Caesar is assassinated.

CAESAR, ALONG WITH his entourage of friends and conspirators, encounter the soothsayer on their way to the Capitol. Implying that the soothsayer was wrong in his warning, Caesar remarks to him that the Ides of March has come. The soothsayer agrees, but ominously replies that it has not yet gone. Artemidorus steps forward and hands Caesar his letter. Calling it a schedule, he instructs Caesar to read it. Decius hands Caesar another paper, telling him that Trebonius asks for a petition.

Fearing Caesar will not read his warning in time, Artemidorus urges him to read his letter first, since it is relevant to Caesar's personal interest. Caesar magnanimously replies that, if that is the case, he will read it last. Desperate, Artemidorus begs him one last time before he is pressed aside by Publius—a senator and Antony's nephew. As Caesar's party enters the senate house, the senator Popilius Lena moves close to Cassius and wishes him success in his business that day. Cassius asks him to explain himself, but Popilius has already stepped away and approached Caesar. Fearing they have been discovered, Cassius anxiously tells Brutus what Popilius said.

Brutus coolly tells his brother-in-law to observe Popilius speaking with Caesar, noting that Popilius smiles and that Caesar's face remains steady. He concludes they are not discussing the assassination plot. Cassius points out that Trebonius is leading Antony away, according to plan. The remaining conspirators see Metellus approach Caesar to discuss his petition. Knowing this to be their signal, they move in close. Cinna reminds Casca that he will be first to strike Caesar.

Metellus kneels before Caesar and begins his false supplication. Caesar interrupts, saying that flattery will not influence him to rescind the banishment of Metellus' brother. Brutus comes forward and kneels before Caesar. To Caesar's surprise, he kisses Caesar's hand, asking him to repeal the banishment. Cassius kneels presenting the same request. At this, Caesar remarks that his own character is steadfast as the fixed north star. He says that he will demonstrate his constancy by upholding his order of banishment.

The conspirators close in tightly under the pretense of supporting Metellus' petition. Cinna kneels. Decius kneels. Unmoved, Caesar points out that he has even denied Brutus (implying a special love for him) and he urges them to relent. Casca leaps up, stabbing Caesar in the back of the neck and the other conspirators quickly follow. As Brutus inflicts the final wound, Caesar turns to him saying, in essence, "Even you, Brutus? Then I go willingly to my death."

HISTORY
According to *Plutarch's Lives*, Shakespeare's primary source for *Julius Caesar*, Casca gave Caesar only a superficial wound. Caesar grabbed Casca's hand, but finding himself being stabbed by many, he looked around and saw Brutus with his dagger drawn against him. Caesar let go of Casca's hand and, covering his head with his robe, gave himself up to their blows.

ACT 3, SCENE 1 PART 2

Confusion in the senate; Antony postures to the conspirators.

AT CAESAR'S DEATH, the senate house erupts into chaos. Citizens and senators flee the building in fear. Cinna and Cassius cry "Liberty! Freedom! Tyranny is dead!" while Brutus attempts to calm the people. He tells them they need not fear—Caesar's death has paid the debt for his own ambition. Brutus is told that Antony's nephew, Publius, is nearby, completely stunned by the assassination. Brutus reassures Publius as Cassius advises the senator to leave their company for his own safety.

By this time, all have left the building, save the conspirators. Cassius asks where Antony has gone and Trebonius, who led Antony away during the assassination, tells Cassius that he has fled home in astonishment. He continues that everyone is confused, as if it were the end of the world. Brutus orders the others to smear their arms and swords with Caesar's blood and cry out in the marketplace, "Peace, freedom and liberty!" Antony's servant enters and kneels. He requests on behalf of his master the guarantee of a safe meeting with Brutus to find out why Caesar had to die.

Brutus gives his assurance and the servant departs. Brutus is optimistic Antony will come to be their friend, but Cassius expresses his doubts. Antony arrives and, though Brutus greets him enthusiastically, Antony only sees Caesar lying dead. He grieves for Caesar, glorifying his accomplishments while at the same time using words deliberately calculated to curry favor with the conspirators.

Antony tells them that if they intend to kill him also, then there is no better time—the hour of Caesar's death. Brutus tells him not to ask for death, but to be patient while they address the people of Rome. Antony, ostensibly agreeing with this course of action, shakes hands with each conspirator, telling them he is their ally and loves them.

Brutus assures Antony their reasons for killing Caesar will satisfy him. Antony asks if he may speak at the funeral (the point to his posturing) and Brutus agrees against Cassius' misgivings. Brutus says he will speak first and then announce that Antony is to speak by their permission. He obtains assurance that Antony will not speak against them from the pulpit.

The body of Caesar is left with Antony and, alone, he delivers a moving eulogy, prophesying suffering on Rome and promising vengeance on the conspirators. Octavius' servant enters and informs Antony that his master is seven miles from Rome. Antony instructs him to attend the funeral and then bring Octavius news of the assassination. They leave, carrying the body of Rome's fallen colossus to the marketplace.

POMPEY
Pompey the Great was loved by the people for ending the slave revolt instigated by Spartacus. Later, he formed an alliance with Caesar and Crassus, referred to as the First Triumvirate. When jealousies arose, Pompey changed political parties against Caesar, and was defeated by him in Greece. Caesar ironically died at the foot of his rival's statue.

ACT 3, SCENES 2 & 3

Brutus and Antony speak at Caesar's funeral; the citizens riot.

CITIZENS OF ROME follow Brutus and Cassius into the street, demanding an explanation for the assassination. Brutus divides the crowd and sends Cassius with one group to another street. Brutus ascends the Forum pulpit and begins by invoking his own honor in an appeal for their trust. He proclaims that although he loved Caesar no less than any of Caesar's friends, he loved Rome more. He asks if they would rather Caesar live and they die slaves, or Caesar die and they live free.

Brutus says that, while he rejoiced in Caesar's fortune, his death was necessary to cut off his ambition. Brutus continues his reasoned oration by asking if anyone is so coarse that they would allow themselves to become a slave, or if anyone is so immoral that they do not love their country. The plebeians respond that none of them are. Antony approaches, dragging a coffin containing the corpse of Caesar. Brutus tells them that Antony had no hand in Caesar's death, but will reap the benefits of it. He concludes by offering to kill himself if the people require it. They respond emphatically, "Live!" and attempt to crown Brutus, offering to carry him home. He tells them to listen to Antony.

Mingling doubt with his impersonal praises for the conspirators, Antony begins his brilliant funeral oration. He frequently refers to the conspirators as "honorable men," so much so that the crowd begins to question the statement's veracity. He casts doubt on Brutus' accusation that Caesar was overly ambitious, bringing to mind Caesar's refusal of the crown at the Lupercalia games. He reminds the crowd that they did love Caesar once and asks what prevents them from mourning Caesar now. Antony pauses for his tears. As he does so, the citizens shift their sympathies from Brutus to Antony. Producing Caesar's will, he says the crowd would riot if he were to read it. The plebeians demand Antony read the will, but he coyly refuses.

They persist in their demands. Antony responds by pointing out each hole in Caesar's cloak, naming the conspirator who inflicted it. As the people weep, Antony lifts the cloak to reveal Caesar's body. Incensed, the people call for revenge. Antony then reads the will, which leaves property and money to the Roman people. The crowd rushes off to burn the houses of the conspirators with brands from Caesar's funeral pyre.

Octavius' servant finds Antony and informs him that Octavius is with Lepidus at Caesar's house and that Brutus and Cassius have fled the city. The riotous throng comes upon Cinna the poet, who quickly explains he is not Cinna the conspirator. Unswayed by details, the people carry the unlucky namesake off to die "for his bad verses."

PLEBEIANS
The fickle plebeians in *Julius Caesar* are a Shakespearean invention. They are treated poorly by the nobility: first they are accosted by the two tribunes, then they are manipulated into rioting by Antony's speech and later they are lied to when their legacy from Caesar is reduced by the triumvirs to fund the war.

ACT 4, SCENE 1

The triumvirs Octavius, Antony and Lepidus proscribe their enemies.

ANTONY, OCTAVIUS AND LEPIDUS have gathered at Antony's house in Rome. These three men form a new triumvirate, having divided among themselves Rome's possessions throughout the world. As the scene begins, their meeting is nearly over. Antony pronounces that the names marked on his list shall be condemned. Octavius turns to Lepidus and remarks that Lepidus' brother is among those set down to die. He asks him for his consent to the execution.

As Lepidus agrees, he is interrupted by Octavius' hastily ordering Antony to mark it down. Lepidus continues, saying his agreement is contingent on the surety that Antony's nephew, Publius, also be condemned. Antony consents and marks a spot next to his name. Looking up from the list, Antony tells Lepidus to go to Caesar's house and bring back the will so they may strategize how best to reduce the payment of Caesar's bequests to the citizens of Rome. Lepidus asks if the two will still be at Antony's house when he returns. Octavius answers that they will be either there or at the Capitol. Lepidus departs on his errand.

Immediately after his departure, Antony comments that Lepidus is an ordinary man, useful only for sending on errands. He expresses doubt as to whether Lepidus is fit to control one third of the empire. Octavius reminds Antony of a prior conversation (not seen in the play) wherein he believed Lepidus was suitable for the task. Even now, he points out, Antony took Lepidus' advice on who should be condemned in their proscription.

Antony reminds the younger Octavius of their age difference. He goes on to say that Lepidus bears the honorable title of triumvir like a beast bears a precious burden—without knowledge of its value. Octavius laconically defends Lepidus, calling him an experienced and brave soldier. Antony then compares Lepidus to his horse,

who is himself brave and experienced in warfare. He argues his horse was taught to fight, just as Lepidus was and, like Lepidus, has no initiative apart from his master. He advises Octavius to think of Lepidus only as a commodity to be used.

Turning the subject to more pressing matters, Antony explains to Octavius that Brutus and Cassius are building armies. Urging expediency, he suggests they combine their forces, gather their allies and make the most of their means for war. He recommends they assemble a council to discuss espionage and strategies. Octavius agrees and, using the metaphor of bear baiting (a popular pastime in Elizabethan culture) reminds Antony they are surrounded by men who cannot be trusted.

TRIUMVIRATE
A great political alliance, the first triumvirate was composed of Julius Caesar, Pompey the Great and Marcus Crassus, for the purpose of extending the scope of their influence against the senate. It dissolved when political differences arose between Caesar and Pompey.

ACT 4.2 & 4.3, PART 1

The armies of Cassius and Brutus join at Sardis; the argument begins.

JUST OUTSIDE the city of Sardis, Brutus and his army prepare to meet up with Cassius and his army. Brutus asks his friend and ally Lucilius if his brother-in-law is nearby. Lucilius replies that he is and that Pindarus, his bondservant, has come to greet Brutus. Brutus is pleased by the greeting. He tells Pindarus that his master, Cassius, has given Brutus reason to wish they had not done some of the things they did. He requests an explanation.

Pindarus assures Brutus that he will be satisfied. Brutus then takes Lucilius aside and inquires how Cassius has treated him. Lucilius informs Brutus that Cassius was courteous and respectful, but not as friendly as in times past. Brutus comments that he is describing friendship that has cooled off. He looks up to find that Cassius has arrived, as Cassius' army rides up to meet Brutus. Immediately Cassius accuses Brutus of wronging him. Brutus reacts dramatically, saying that he does not even wrong his enemies, let alone a brother. When Cassius presses his accusation, Brutus suggests they move into his tent, out of hearing of the armies.

With Lucius and Titinius set to guard the door—and Lucilius nearby—Brutus and Cassius enter the tent. Cassius elaborates on his complaint, saying Brutus condemned a man named Lucius Pella for accepting bribes, ignoring Cassius' letters to the contrary. Brutus says that Cassius soiled his own reputation to write on behalf of such a man. He goes on to say that Cassius is considered greedy because he trades officership in his army for money. Cassius counters that if any man other than Brutus had said these things, those words would be his last.

Brutus' intellective idealism clashes with Cassius' pragmatic realism. Reminding Cassius of the assassination, Brutus asks who among them stabbed Caesar if not for justice. Shall they then, he continues, contaminate their hands with bribes and sell their offices for money? Cassius demands that Brutus not provoke him. He claims to be a more experienced soldier and better general than Brutus. Brutus tells him to go make his servants afraid. Cassius complains that not even Caesar would have angered him this way. Brutus says that Cassius dared not tempt Caesar. He continues, saying he is not afraid of Cassius' threats. He points out that his honesty prevents him from raising money in corrupt ways, but when he asked Cassius for a sum of money, he was refused. Cassius denies refusing Brutus, saying the messenger who refused Brutus the money was a fool and he accuses Brutus of no longer loving him. Insultingly, Brutus says he doesn't dislike Cassius, he dislikes Cassius' enormous faults.

INTEGRITY
Although Brutus frequently reminds the other characters (and the audience) of his infallible integrity, a moral dilemma exists in this scene. Brutus cites that Cassius had denied him money. At the same time he condemns Cassius for extortion. Brutus considers himself far too honorable to perform the actual extortion himself, but not so honorable that he is above accepting money originating through such means.

ACT 4, SCENE 3 PART 2

The reconciliation of Brutus and Cassius; Caesar's ghost appears.

AT BRUTUS' MENTION of Cassius' faults, Cassius cries out to their enemies, Antony and Octavius, to exact their revenge on Cassius alone. Saying he is weary of the world in which he is hated by his brother, he offers Brutus his dagger. Brushing the gesture aside, Brutus tells Cassius to put the dagger away. He assures Cassius that he is now quiet as a lamb, saying his anger is like a spark that flares up and is gone in a moment.

Cassius asks rhetorically if he has lived to see the day when Brutus would make him the brunt of jokes. Brutus admits he only said that out of anger. Seizing the opportunity for amends, Cassius extends his hand. Brutus says he gives his heart as well and the two reconcile. They hear a man outside the tent insisting on seeing the generals. Lucilius tries to restrain the man, but he forces his way inside. It is a poet who speaks a short, clumsy verse shaming Brutus and Cassius for arguing and admonishing them to love one another. The two men laugh at the inept rhyme and summarily toss the poet out of the tent.

Lucilius and Titinius are ordered to to bring Messala to the tent. Cassius comments to Brutus on how angry Brutus was. He says Brutus must have forgotten his Stoic philosophy teaching. Brutus tells Cassius that Portia is dead. Aghast, Cassius asks how Brutus kept from killing him during their argument. He asks of what sickness Portia died. Brutus answers that she was anxious over his absence and afraid of Antony and Octavius' growing power, so she swallowed hot coals. Changing the subject, he proposes they drink to their reconciliation.

Titinius enters the tent along with Messala. Brutus tells Messala of letters he received reporting on Antony and Octavius' approach with a mighty army. Messala confirms that he, too, has received that report along with news that the triumvirs have executed a hundred senators. Messala also brings news of Portia's death. Both Messala and Cassius comment on Brutus' Stoic ability to bear the loss of his wife. Brutus turns the discussion to their battle strategy. After some dispute, Brutus prevails (possibly because Cassius sympathizes with Brutus' bereavement) and they agree to advance toward the enemy at Philippi—Brutus final blunder.

Varro, Claudius and Lucius sleep in Brutus' tent, but sleep escapes Brutus. Late into the night, the ghost of Caesar appears to him. Brutus asks who he is and the ghost replies, "Thy evil spirit, Brutus." He says they will meet again at Philippi and then vanishes, a foreshadow of Brutus' looming fate.

POETS
The function of poets in ancient times is that of historian. This would explain the presence of a poet in an army camp on the eve of battle. Often these poets would skip to their rhyme, which explains Brutus' reference to "jigging fools." This poet's rhyme is so bad that, according to Plutarch, Cassius fell to laughing and Brutus summarily threw him out of his tent.

ACT 5, SCENE 1

The generals parley at Philippi; Preparations for battle are made.

ON THE PLAINS at Philippi, Octavius expresses his satisfaction to Antony that the enemy is coming to meet them. He reminds Antony of a conversation in which Antony said Brutus and Cassius would keep to the hills. Antony says he now knows what is in their thoughts. He explains that the armies of Brutus and Cassius plan to make a brave show of force by descending on them from the hills. He says they mean to instill a sense of fear, but that it will not work.

A messenger comes to them with urgent news: the enemy is approaching, displaying red flags of battle. Antony instructs Octavius to lead his troops to the left side of the field. Octavius replies that he will go to the right side and tells Antony to keep to the left. When Antony asks why his colleague is countering his judgment at this crucial time, Octavius says he is not disagreeing with him, but that he will still go to the right. (Octavius—or Augustus, as he is later conferred—was historically known as a cold, politically-adept, equanimous man; Shakespeare shows these traits in this scene and previously in 4.1.)

Brutus and Cassius approach with their army, which includes their friends Lucilius, Titinius and Messala. Brutus notes that the presence of the opposing generals signals a parley. Octavius asks Antony if they should give the order to attack, but Antony advises they respond to the generals, implying they should answer the verbal assaults first.

Brutus speaks first and, purposely twisting a proverb, asks rhetorically if they will exchange words before exchanging blows. Immediately the conversation explodes with recriminations. Antony says that Brutus had good words before stabbing Caesar. Cassius points out that they would not need to listen to Antony if Brutus had listened to Cassius months ago. Octavius draws his sword against the conspirators and says it will not be put away until Caesar is avenged. He leads Antony away while hurling threats at Brutus and Cassius.

As Brutus meets with Lucilius, Cassius speaks to Messala. He tells Messala that it is his birthday. He says they have foolishly placed all their hopes on one single battle and now the gathering birds look down on them as if they are nearly dead. Messala tries to encourage him and Brutus returns. Cassius tells him they should say their farewells in case they lose the battle. Brutus says that this battle will end the work begun on the Ides of March. He and Cassius exchange touching farewells before riding off to join their armies, preparing for the battle that will soon decide their destiny.

GLADIATORS
Brutus' fugitive status rendered him unable to raise a legitimate army. He and Cassius were forced to resort to gladiators and hired officers. Their armies were up against those of Antony and Octavius which were highly-trained, numerically-superior Roman legions.

ACT 5, SCENES 2 & 3

The battle begins; Cassius commits suicide due to an erroneous report.

AMID THE CLAMOR of battle, Brutus gives Messala a handful of documents containing his instructions. He orders him to ride quickly and deliver them to the forces on the other side of the valley. As the battle sounds intensify, Brutus reveals his plans: they are to advance immediately because he perceives fear in the ranks of Octavius. He says that a sudden show of force will overthrow the enemy. They depart in opposite directions.

In another part of the field, Cassius laments to Titinius that his own soldiers are attempting to desert him. Titinius tells him Brutus gave orders to advance too early and his soldiers are looting while Cassius' army is surrounded by Antony's. Pindarus runs to them, warning them to flee. He tells them that Antony has advanced to their tents. The three men flee to a hill, where Cassius stops them. Seeing men surrounding his burning tents, he tells Titinius to ride and report back on whether the men are allies or enemies. Titinius promises a swift return.

Confessing weak eyesight, Cassius sends his bondservant Pindarus up the hill to report what he sees. As Pindarus ascends, Cassius says it is his birthday and he now believes his life has run its course. From above, Pindarus reports (incorrectly) that Titinius has been surrounded by horsemen, who dismount and take him captive. As Pindarus and Cassius hear shouts of joy, Cassius sadly tells Pindarus to come down. He labels himself a coward to have watched while his best friend is taken captive. Not waiting for the possibility of a verified report, Cassius calls his bondservant and reminds him of the day he took him prisoner, making him swear to do whatever Cassius asked. Handing his sword to Pindarus, he pronounces him a free man. Cassius covers his face and guides the sword as his master runs on it, killing himself. Pindarus says he would not have wanted to be freed like this and runs away.

Titinius returns with Messala, who comments that the battles have ended in a draw—Brutus has defeated Octavius, while Antony has defeated Cassius. They discover Cassius' body on the ground and Titinius delivers a touching eulogy. Messala leaves to inform Brutus. Alone, Titinius reveals that he wasn't captured, but met with Brutus' men who gave him a victory wreath. After placing it on Cassius' head, Titinius stabs himself. Messala returns with Brutus and Young Cato. They see the two men on the ground and Brutus commends them both as the best of Romans before returning to his army.

INTERPRETATION
A theme of interpretation runs throughout *Julius Caesar*. The storm in 1.3 is taken by Casca for a bad omen, but Cicero says that men will interpret things as they see fit. In 2.2 Decius reinterprets Calpurnia's dream. In this scene it takes on tragic consequences as Pindarus misinterprets the shouts of joy from Brutus' men as shouts of victory from Antony's soldiers, leading to Cassius' hasty suicide.

ACT 5, SCENES 4 & 5

The second battle at Philippi; the death of Marcus Brutus.

AS THE FIGHTING rages in the second battle, Brutus calls encouragement to his overrun army and moves on. Young Cato takes up the battle cry, shouting his name on the field and proclaiming his patriotism. In an effort to gain Brutus time to flee, Lucilius announces that he is Brutus, a friend of Rome. The soldiers quickly overtake Young Cato and kill him. Lucilius speaks to him touchingly, saying that he died bravely and will be honored.

A soldier approaches and demands Lucilius surrender. Lucilius responds that he will only surrender to death. He offers the soldier money to kill him, saying, "Kill Brutus, and be honored in his death." The soldier says he cannot kill so valuable a prisoner and he takes Lucilius captive. As Antony approaches, the soldiers announce Brutus' capture. Antony asks to see him and Lucilius—knowing Antony will not be fooled—says that Brutus will never allow himself to be taken alive. Antony tells the soldiers that their prisoner is not Brutus, but is a noble captive nonetheless. He orders Lucilius be treated with kindness.

The final scene of the play begins as the retreating Brutus stops to rest with a handful of his remaining friends. Brutus whispers to his servant Clitus, who reacts in shock. He refuses Brutus' unheard request, saying he would not do it for the world. Brutus then whispers to Dardanius, who responds in like manner. The two servants quietly ask one another what Brutus requested and discover that he asked them both to kill him.

Brutus strikes up a conversation with Volumnius, telling him of the appearances of Caesar's ghost, first at Sardis (seen in 4.3) and next on the previous night. Citing their long friendship, Brutus asks Volumnius to hold his sword while Brutus runs on it. Volumnius refuses, saying it is not a task for a friend. The sounds of battle grow louder and Clitus calls for them to flee. Brutus wakes his servant Strato, who had fallen asleep, and sends his friends on ahead, asking Strato to stay behind. He bids his servant to hold his sword and in a gesture of intimacy, the servant responds by taking Brutus' hand as well. Brutus runs on the sword and, with his dying breath, affirms that he killed Caesar half as willingly as himself.

Octavius and Antony enter with Messala and Lucilius. They discover from Strato that Brutus has died. On Messala's recommendation, Octavius takes Strato into his service. Antony calls Brutus the noblest Roman. Octavius announces that Brutus will be buried with all respect and honor. He then calls the battlefield to rest as the play comes to a close.

FRIENDSHIP
According to Plutarch, Brutus pleads with Volumnius for the sake of the philosophy they've read as adults, which he claims resulted in their acquaintance. In the play, Shakespeare changes the reference, portraying Brutus and Volumnius as childhood schoolfriends. In this manner, a more intimate connection is created to contrast with the violence of battle.

APPENDIX A:
DRAMATIC MAPS

The Dramatic Maps that follow are schematic representations of *Julius Caesar* by scene. In each case, the main ideas of the scene are highlighted on the timeline, alongside their initial corresponding line number. The brackets attempt larger groupings of the ideas to provide a sense of the overall movement of the scene. The line numbers of Shakespeare's *Julius Caesar* differ greatly between Quartos, Folios and consequently, publishers—each publishing is an interpretive work. Keep in mind they are guidelines for general assistance; your specific version may vary.

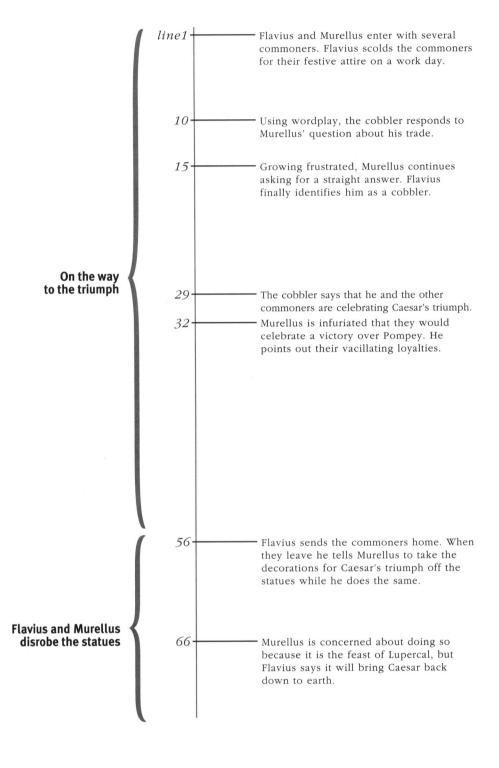

1.1

line 1 — Flavius and Murellus enter with several commoners. Flavius scolds the commoners for their festive attire on a work day.

10 — Using wordplay, the cobbler responds to Murellus' question about his trade.

15 — Growing frustrated, Murellus continues asking for a straight answer. Flavius finally identifies him as a cobbler.

On the way to the triumph

29 — The cobbler says that he and the other commoners are celebrating Caesar's triumph.

32 — Murellus is infuriated that they would celebrate a victory over Pompey. He points out their vacillating loyalties.

56 — Flavius sends the commoners home. When they leave he tells Murellus to take the decorations for Caesar's triumph off the statues while he does the same.

Flavius and Murellus disrobe the statues

66 — Murellus is concerned about doing so because it is the feast of Lupercal, but Flavius says it will bring Caesar back down to earth.

Caesar and his entourage enter. Caesar —————— *line 1*
tells Antony to touch Calpurnia as he
races to free her from infertility.
A soothsayer calls out to Caesar: "Beware —————— *20*
the Ides of March." Caesar calls him a
dreamer and dismisses him. Everyone
leaves except Cassius and Brutus.

A warning for Caesar

Cassius points out the high regard that the —————— *56*
Romans have for Brutus and that many
complain about the current government.

The two hear trumpets and shouts from —————— *81*
the crowd. Brutus fears the people have
made Caesar king. Cassius says that
Caesar is no better than he or Brutus.

Concern for Rome

They hear another shout from the
crowd. Brutus says they may have
given Caesar some new honor. —————— *133*

Cassius expresses his dislike of one man —————— *150*
having so much power in Rome. Brutus
agrees to discuss it with him later.

Caesar returns with his entourage. —————— *178*
Brutus notes that he looks angry.

Caesar, talking only to Antony, says that —————— *194*
Cassius is dangerous, but he doesn't fear him.

Caesar and his group exit. Casca, who stays —————— *216*
behind, tells Brutus that the crowd cheered
when Caesar refused the crown
offered to him by Antony.

Caesar's anger

Casca exits. Brutus invites Cassius to speak
with him the next day. Brutus exits. —————— *289*

Alone, Cassius says that Brutus may be —————— *303*
convinced. He contrives to forge letters extolling
Brutus and alluding to Caesar's ambition.

Cassius' plan

1.3

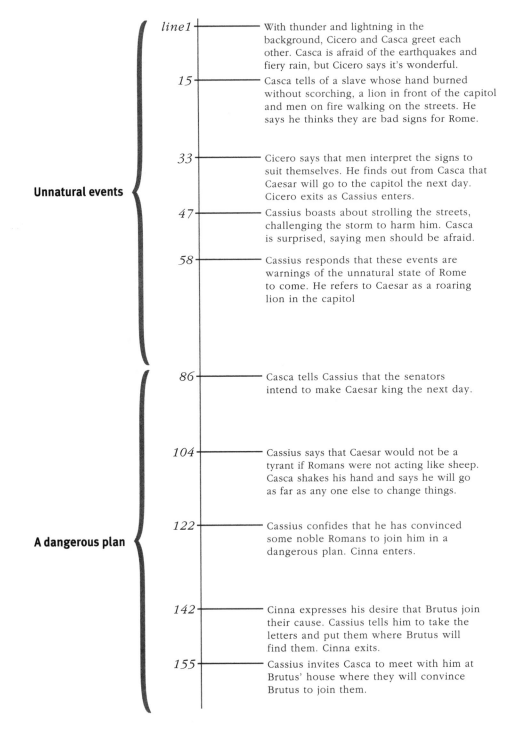

Unnatural events

line 1 — With thunder and lightning in the background, Cicero and Casca greet each other. Casca is afraid of the earthquakes and fiery rain, but Cicero says it's wonderful.

15 — Casca tells of a slave whose hand burned without scorching, a lion in front of the capitol and men on fire walking on the streets. He says he thinks they are bad signs for Rome.

33 — Cicero says that men interpret the signs to suit themselves. He finds out from Casca that Caesar will go to the capitol the next day. Cicero exits as Cassius enters.

47 — Cassius boasts about strolling the streets, challenging the storm to harm him. Casca is surprised, saying men should be afraid.

58 — Cassius responds that these events are warnings of the unnatural state of Rome to come. He refers to Caesar as a roaring lion in the capitol

86 — Casca tells Cassius that the senators intend to make Caesar king the next day.

104 — Cassius says that Caesar would not be a tyrant if Romans were not acting like sheep. Casca shakes his hand and says he will go as far as any one else to change things.

A dangerous plan

122 — Cassius confides that he has convinced some noble Romans to join him in a dangerous plan. Cinna enters.

142 — Cinna expresses his desire that Brutus join their cause. Cassius tells him to take the letters and put them where Brutus will find them. Cinna exits.

155 — Cassius invites Casca to meet with him at Brutus' house where they will convince Brutus to join them.

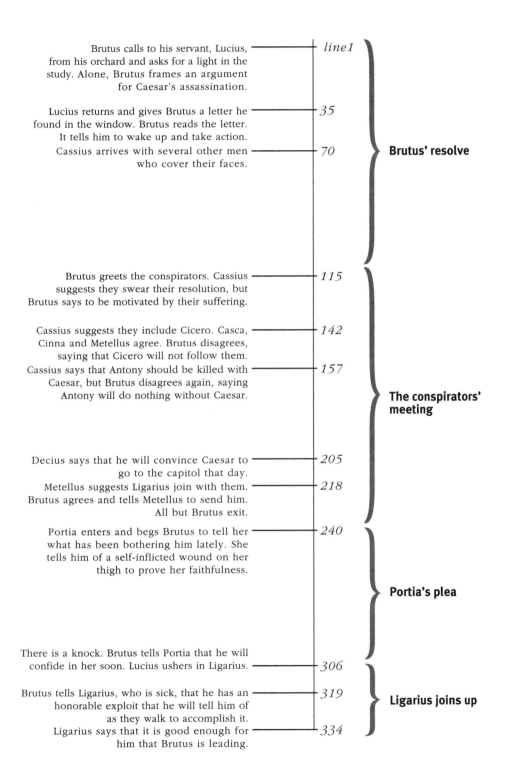

Brutus calls to his servant, Lucius, from his orchard and asks for a light in the study. Alone, Brutus frames an argument for Caesar's assassination. — line 1

Lucius returns and gives Brutus a letter he found in the window. Brutus reads the letter. It tells him to wake up and take action. — 35

Cassius arrives with several other men who cover their faces. — 70

Brutus' resolve

Brutus greets the conspirators. Cassius suggests they swear their resolution, but Brutus says to be motivated by their suffering. — 115

Cassius suggests they include Cicero. Casca, Cinna and Metellus agree. Brutus disagrees, saying that Cicero will not follow them. — 142

Cassius says that Antony should be killed with Caesar, but Brutus disagrees again, saying Antony will do nothing without Caesar. — 157

The conspirators' meeting

Decius says that he will convince Caesar to go to the capitol that day. — 205

Metellus suggests Ligarius join with them. Brutus agrees and tells Metellus to send him. All but Brutus exit. — 218

Portia enters and begs Brutus to tell her what has been bothering him lately. She tells him of a self-inflicted wound on her thigh to prove her faithfulness. — 240

Portia's plea

There is a knock. Brutus tells Portia that he will confide in her soon. Lucius ushers in Ligarius. — 306

Brutus tells Ligarius, who is sick, that he has an honorable exploit that he will tell him of as they walk to accomplish it. — 319

Ligarius says that it is good enough for him that Brutus is leading. — 334

Ligarius joins up

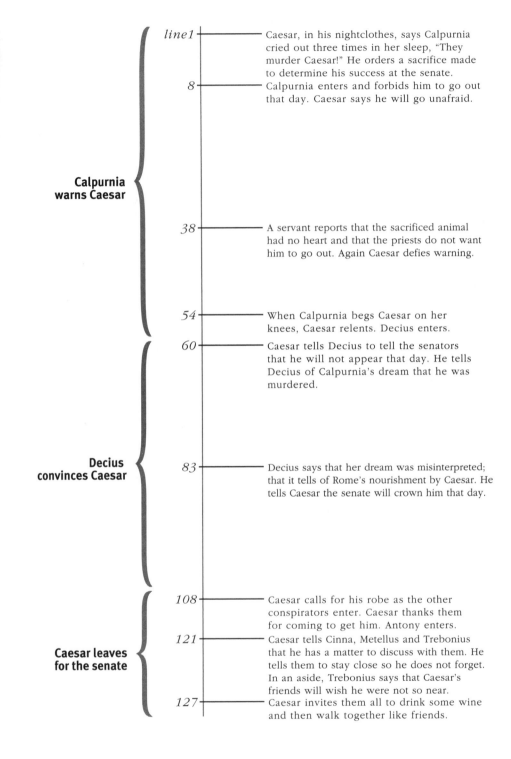

**Calpurnia
warns Caesar**

line 1 — Caesar, in his nightclothes, says Calpurnia cried out three times in her sleep, "They murder Caesar!" He orders a sacrifice made to determine his success at the senate.

8 — Calpurnia enters and forbids him to go out that day. Caesar says he will go unafraid.

38 — A servant reports that the sacrificed animal had no heart and that the priests do not want him to go out. Again Caesar defies warning.

54 — When Calpurnia begs Caesar on her knees, Caesar relents. Decius enters.

**Decius
convinces Caesar**

60 — Caesar tells Decius to tell the senators that he will not appear that day. He tells Decius of Calpurnia's dream that he was murdered.

83 — Decius says that her dream was misinterpreted; that it tells of Rome's nourishment by Caesar. He tells Caesar the senate will crown him that day.

**Caesar leaves
for the senate**

108 — Caesar calls for his robe as the other conspirators enter. Caesar thanks them for coming to get him. Antony enters.

121 — Caesar tells Cinna, Metellus and Trebonius that he has a matter to discuss with them. He tells them to stay close so he does not forget. In an aside, Trebonius says that Caesar's friends will wish he were not so near.

127 — Caesar invites them all to drink some wine and then walk together like friends.

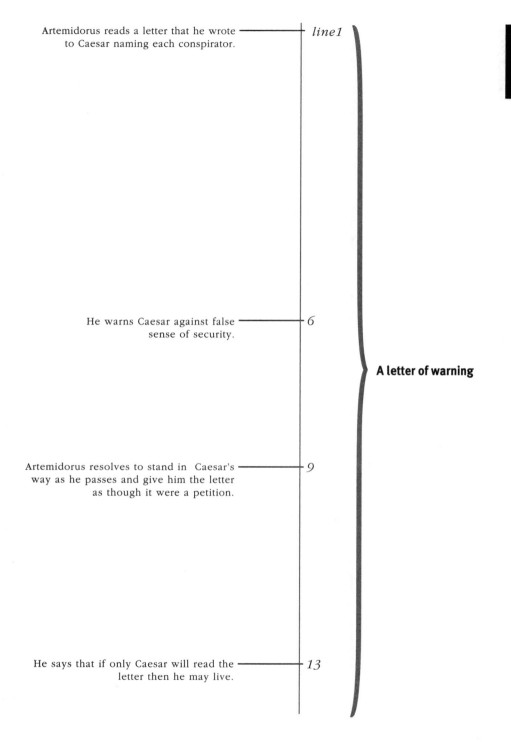

Artemidorus reads a letter that he wrote ———— *line1*
to Caesar naming each conspirator.

He warns Caesar against false ———— *6*
sense of security.

A letter of warning

Artemidorus resolves to stand in Caesar's ———— *9*
way as he passes and give him the letter
as though it were a petition.

He says that if only Caesar will read the ———— *13*
letter then he may live.

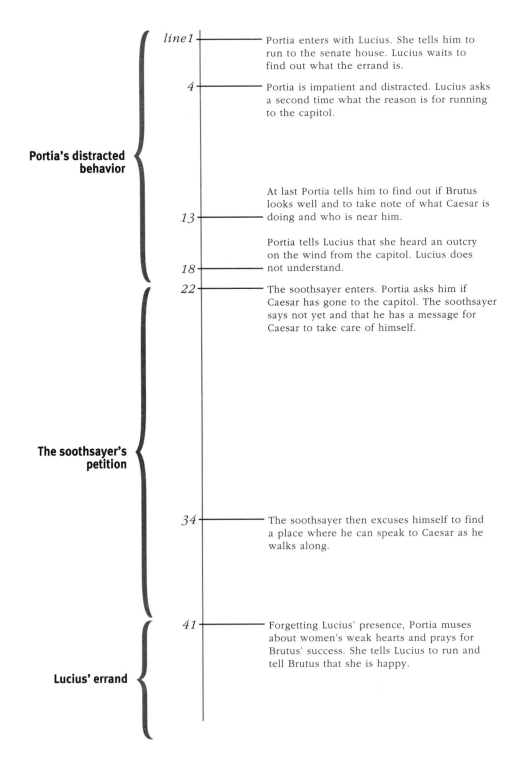

line1 — Portia enters with Lucius. She tells him to run to the senate house. Lucius waits to find out what the errand is.

4 — Portia is impatient and distracted. Lucius asks a second time what the reason is for running to the capitol.

Portia's distracted behavior

13 — At last Portia tells him to find out if Brutus looks well and to take note of what Caesar is doing and who is near him.

18 — Portia tells Lucius that she heard an outcry on the wind from the capitol. Lucius does not understand.

22 — The soothsayer enters. Portia asks him if Caesar has gone to the capitol. The soothsayer says not yet and that he has a message for Caesar to take care of himself.

The soothsayer's petition

34 — The soothsayer then excuses himself to find a place where he can speak to Caesar as he walks along.

41 — Forgetting Lucius' presence, Portia muses about women's weak hearts and prays for Brutus' success. She tells Lucius to run and tell Brutus that she is happy.

Lucius' errand

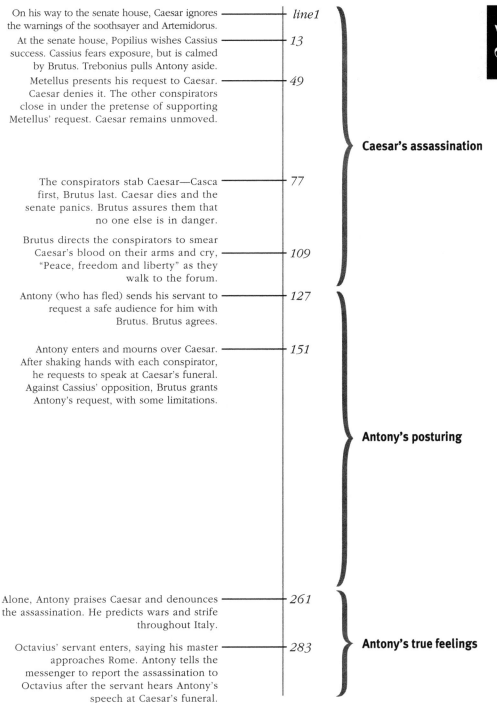

On his way to the senate house, Caesar ignores the warnings of the soothsayer and Artemidorus. — *line1*

At the senate house, Popilius wishes Cassius success. Cassius fears exposure, but is calmed by Brutus. Trebonius pulls Antony aside. — *13*

Metellus presents his request to Caesar. Caesar denies it. The other conspirators close in under the pretense of supporting Metellus' request. Caesar remains unmoved. — *49*

Caesar's assassination

The conspirators stab Caesar—Casca first, Brutus last. Caesar dies and the senate panics. Brutus assures them that no one else is in danger. — *77*

Brutus directs the conspirators to smear Caesar's blood on their arms and cry, "Peace, freedom and liberty" as they walk to the forum. — *109*

Antony (who has fled) sends his servant to request a safe audience for him with Brutus. Brutus agrees. — *127*

Antony enters and mourns over Caesar. After shaking hands with each conspirator, he requests to speak at Caesar's funeral. Against Cassius' opposition, Brutus grants Antony's request, with some limitations. — *151*

Antony's posturing

Alone, Antony praises Caesar and denounces the assassination. He predicts wars and strife throughout Italy. — *261*

Octavius' servant enters, saying his master approaches Rome. Antony tells the messenger to report the assassination to Octavius after the servant hears Antony's speech at Caesar's funeral. — *283*

Antony's true feelings

3.1

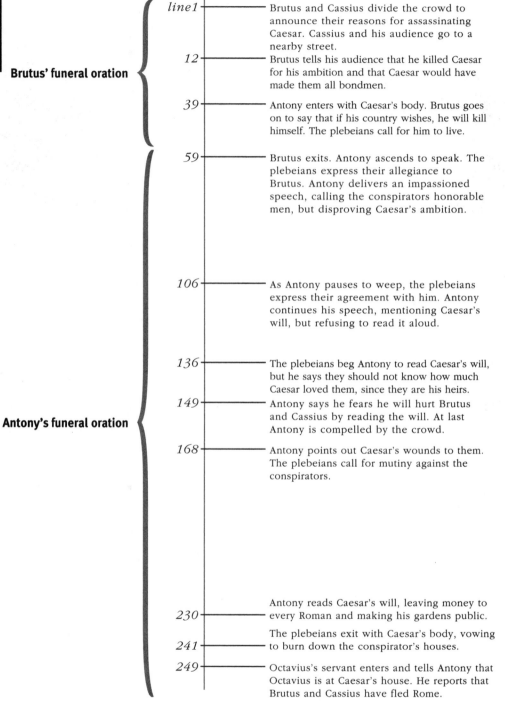

3.2

Brutus' funeral oration

line1 — Brutus and Cassius divide the crowd to announce their reasons for assassinating Caesar. Cassius and his audience go to a nearby street.

12 — Brutus tells his audience that he killed Caesar for his ambition and that Caesar would have made them all bondmen.

39 — Antony enters with Caesar's body. Brutus goes on to say that if his country wishes, he will kill himself. The plebeians call for him to live.

Antony's funeral oration

59 — Brutus exits. Antony ascends to speak. The plebeians express their allegiance to Brutus. Antony delivers an impassioned speech, calling the conspirators honorable men, but disproving Caesar's ambition.

106 — As Antony pauses to weep, the plebeians express their agreement with him. Antony continues his speech, mentioning Caesar's will, but refusing to read it aloud.

136 — The plebeians beg Antony to read Caesar's will, but he says they should not know how much Caesar loved them, since they are his heirs.

149 — Antony says he fears he will hurt Brutus and Cassius by reading the will. At last Antony is compelled by the crowd.

168 — Antony points out Caesar's wounds to them. The plebeians call for mutiny against the conspirators.

230 — Antony reads Caesar's will, leaving money to every Roman and making his gardens public.

241 — The plebeians exit with Caesar's body, vowing to burn down the conspirator's houses.

249 — Octavius's servant enters and tells Antony that Octavius is at Caesar's house. He reports that Brutus and Cassius have fled Rome.

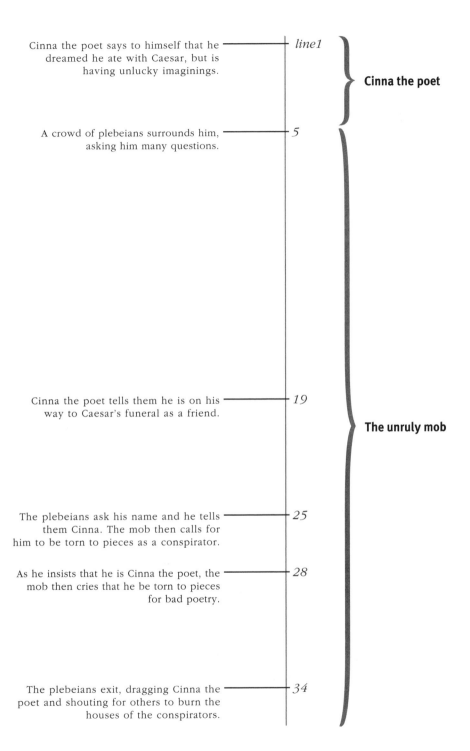

Cinna the poet says to himself that he dreamed he ate with Caesar, but is having unlucky imaginings. — *line1*

} **Cinna the poet**

A crowd of plebeians surrounds him, asking him many questions. — 5

Cinna the poet tells them he is on his way to Caesar's funeral as a friend. — 19

} **The unruly mob**

The plebeians ask his name and he tells them Cinna. The mob then calls for him to be torn to pieces as a conspirator. — 25

As he insists that he is Cinna the poet, the mob then cries that he be torn to pieces for bad poetry. — 28

The plebeians exit, dragging Cinna the poet and shouting for others to burn the houses of the conspirators. — 34

3.3

4.1

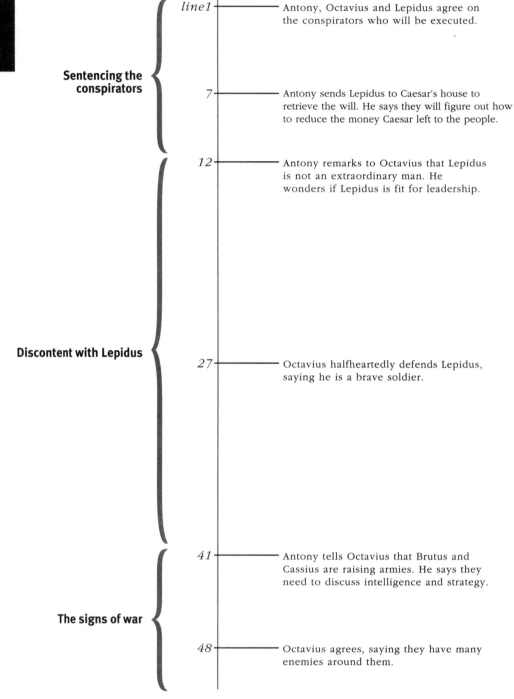

Sentencing the conspirators

line 1 — Antony, Octavius and Lepidus agree on the conspirators who will be executed.

7 — Antony sends Lepidus to Caesar's house to retrieve the will. He says they will figure out how to reduce the money Caesar left to the people.

Discontent with Lepidus

12 — Antony remarks to Octavius that Lepidus is not an extraordinary man. He wonders if Lepidus is fit for leadership.

27 — Octavius halfheartedly defends Lepidus, saying he is a brave soldier.

The signs of war

41 — Antony tells Octavius that Brutus and Cassius are raising armies. He says they need to discuss intelligence and strategy.

48 — Octavius agrees, saying they have many enemies around them.

Brutus and his army, including Lucilius enter ——————— *line 1*
and are greeted by Titinius and Pindarus.

Brutus tells Pindarus that his master Cassius ——————— *6*
has given him a reason to wish they did
not do some of the things they did.

Brutus takes Lucilius aside and asks how
Cassius treated him. Lucilius responds that
Cassius treated him with courtesy, but not
familiarity, as he had previously. ——————— *14*

Brutus tells Lucilius that Cassius is acting ——————— *18*
like a friend who has grown cold.

A friendship cools off

Cassius arrives with his army and tells ——————— *31*
Brutus that Brutus has wronged him.

Brutus denies this and tells Cassius they ——————— *38*
must not speak in front of the troops.

They decide to go into Brutus' tent and talk. ——————— *45*

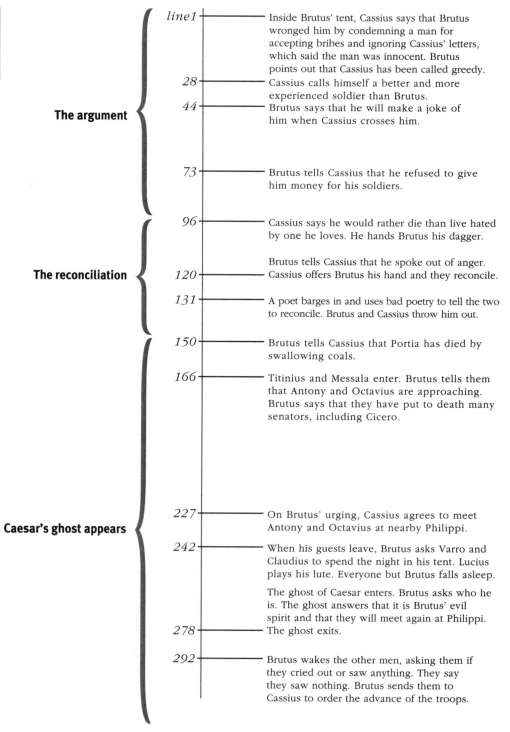

The argument

line 1 — Inside Brutus' tent, Cassius says that Brutus wronged him by condemning a man for accepting bribes and ignoring Cassius' letters, which said the man was innocent. Brutus points out that Cassius has been called greedy.

28 — Cassius calls himself a better and more experienced soldier than Brutus.

44 — Brutus says that he will make a joke of him when Cassius crosses him.

73 — Brutus tells Cassius that he refused to give him money for his soldiers.

The reconciliation

96 — Cassius says he would rather die than live hated by one he loves. He hands Brutus his dagger.

Brutus tells Cassius that he spoke out of anger.

120 — Cassius offers Brutus his hand and they reconcile.

131 — A poet barges in and uses bad poetry to tell the two to reconcile. Brutus and Cassius throw him out.

150 — Brutus tells Cassius that Portia has died by swallowing coals.

166 — Titinius and Messala enter. Brutus tells them that Antony and Octavius are approaching. Brutus says that they have put to death many senators, including Cicero.

Caesar's ghost appears

227 — On Brutus' urging, Cassius agrees to meet Antony and Octavius at nearby Philippi.

242 — When his guests leave, Brutus asks Varro and Claudius to spend the night in his tent. Lucius plays his lute. Everyone but Brutus falls asleep.

The ghost of Caesar enters. Brutus asks who he is. The ghost answers that it is Brutus' evil spirit and that they will meet again at Philippi.

278 — The ghost exits.

292 — Brutus wakes the other men, asking them if they cried out or saw anything. They say they saw nothing. Brutus sends them to Cassius to order the advance of the troops.

Antony and Octavius discuss the enemy's —————— *line1*
advance toward them. A messenger enters
and tells them the battle is near.

Brutus and Cassius enter with their army. —————— *21*
They approach Antony and Octavius and
have an angry conversation with them.

Prelude to battle

Antony and Octavius exit with their army. —————— *66*

Cassius talks with Messala. He tells Messala —————— *71*
that all their hopes lie in this single battle
and that he saw some bad omens.
Messala urges him not to believe it.

Brutus and Cassius exchange final farewells. —————— *114*

A message to advance

line 1 —— Brutus gives a message to Messala to be delivered to Cassius' troops in the distance.

3 —— In the messages, Brutus advises Cassius to advance immediately.

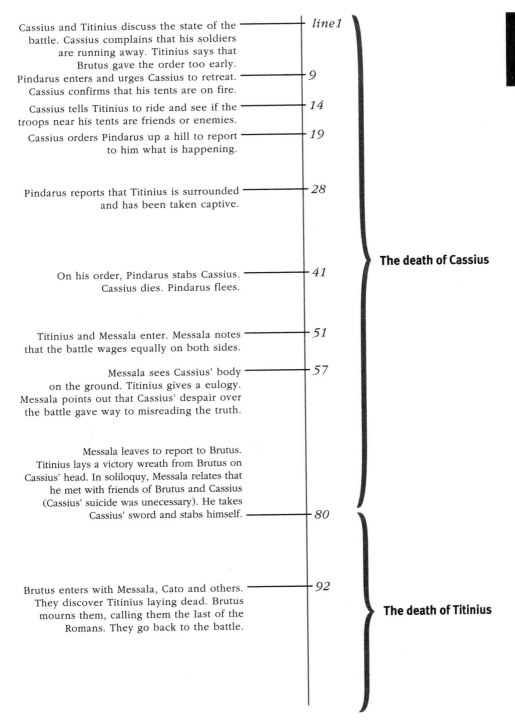

Cassius and Titinius discuss the state of the battle. Cassius complains that his soldiers are running away. Titinius says that Brutus gave the order too early.

line 1

Pindarus enters and urges Cassius to retreat. Cassius confirms that his tents are on fire.

9

Cassius tells Titinius to ride and see if the troops near his tents are friends or enemies.

14

Cassius orders Pindarus up a hill to report to him what is happening.

19

Pindarus reports that Titinius is surrounded and has been taken captive.

28

On his order, Pindarus stabs Cassius. Cassius dies. Pindarus flees.

41

Titinius and Messala enter. Messala notes that the battle wages equally on both sides.

51

Messala sees Cassius' body on the ground. Titinius gives a eulogy. Messala points out that Cassius' despair over the battle gave way to misreading the truth.

57

Messala leaves to report to Brutus. Titinius lays a victory wreath from Brutus on Cassius' head. In soliloquy, Messala relates that he met with friends of Brutus and Cassius (Cassius' suicide was unecessary). He takes Cassius' sword and stabs himself.

80

The death of Cassius

Brutus enters with Messala, Cato and others. They discover Titinius laying dead. Brutus mourns them, calling them the last of the Romans. They go back to the battle.

92

The death of Titinius

5.3

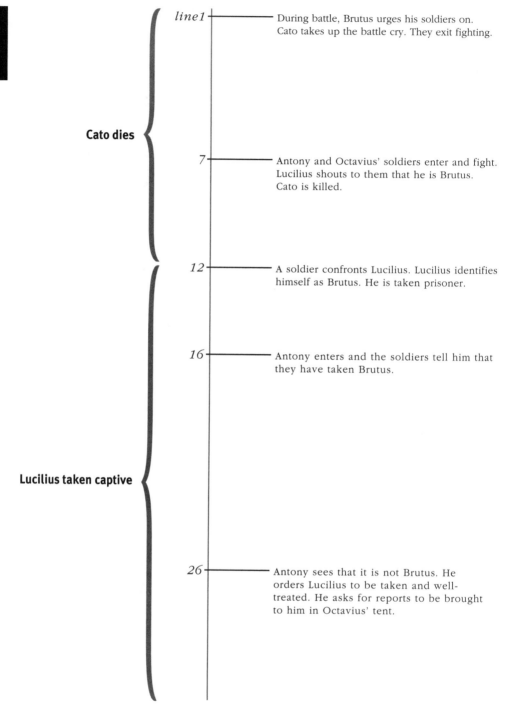

5.4

line1 — During battle, Brutus urges his soldiers on. Cato takes up the battle cry. They exit fighting.

Cato dies

7 — Antony and Octavius' soldiers enter and fight. Lucilius shouts to them that he is Brutus. Cato is killed.

12 — A soldier confronts Lucilius. Lucilius identifies himself as Brutus. He is taken prisoner.

16 — Antony enters and the soldiers tell him that they have taken Brutus.

Lucilius taken captive

26 — Antony sees that it is not Brutus. He orders Lucilius to be taken and well-treated. He asks for reports to be brought to him in Octavius' tent.

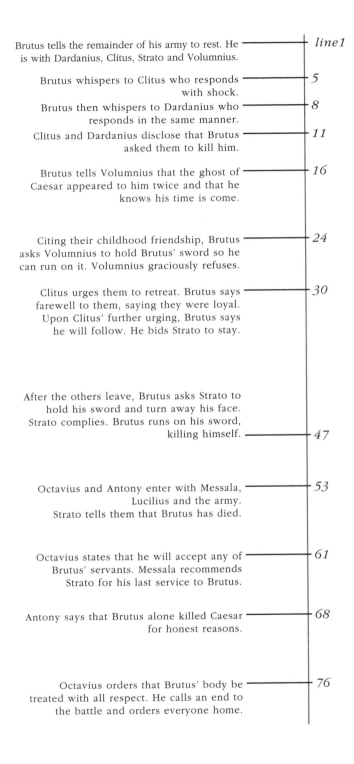

Brutus tells the remainder of his army to rest. He is with Dardanius, Clitus, Strato and Volumnius. — *line 1*

Brutus whispers to Clitus who responds with shock. — *5*

Brutus then whispers to Dardanius who responds in the same manner. — *8*

Clitus and Dardanius disclose that Brutus asked them to kill him. — *11*

Brutus tells Volumnius that the ghost of Caesar appeared to him twice and that he knows his time is come. — *16*

Citing their childhood friendship, Brutus asks Volumnius to hold Brutus' sword so he can run on it. Volumnius graciously refuses. — *24*

Clitus urges them to retreat. Brutus says farewell to them, saying they were loyal. Upon Clitus' further urging, Brutus says he will follow. He bids Strato to stay. — *30*

After the others leave, Brutus asks Strato to hold his sword and turn away his face. Strato complies. Brutus runs on his sword, killing himself. — *47*

The death of Brutus

Octavius and Antony enter with Messala, Lucilius and the army. Strato tells them that Brutus has died. — *53*

Octavius states that he will accept any of Brutus' servants. Messala recommends Strato for his last service to Brutus. — *61*

Antony says that Brutus alone killed Caesar for honest reasons. — *68*

Octavius orders that Brutus' body be treated with all respect. He calls an end to the battle and orders everyone home. — *76*

The end of the war

APPENDIX B:
BACKGROUND

After careful thought we decided to place the background material—generally the first information you see—at the end of the guidebook. The two most compelling reasons for doing so were, first, we did not want to lose the powerful beginning of the opening chapter ("This is Caesar"); and, second, it has been our experience that the background material is usually passed over and then read last anyway. Having said this, we feel that the material in Appendix B is extremely useful to the reader wishing an expanded view of Shakespeare's life as well as sources and nuance relating to *Julius Caesar*.

Shakespeare achieved success in his lifetime.

BUSINESSMAN. Born in 1564—the same year as Galileo—by the time William Shakespeare was 28, he had settled in London as an actor. At 30, he became a shareholder in the Lord Chamberlain's Men, a successful company who often staged plays at court for Queen Elizabeth I.

ACTOR. Shakespeare began as a player and part-time playwright, later focusing all of his energies on writing. He mostly acted character parts—not leading roles—although he is known to have played the character of Old Hamlet's ghost. He received far more income from his acting than from his writing royalties.

PLAYWRIGHT. He is widely regarded as the greatest dramatist of western literature and by some as the greatest thinker. Shakespeare's plays, replete with insights into human character, are performed more often than any other playwright's in history. He achieved success in his own lifetime and, by the time his wife died in 1623, a monument to Shakespeare had been erected in Holy Trinity Church in their hometown of Stratford.

Shakespeare adapted the play from sources.

PLUTARCH: *LIVES OF THE NOBLE GREEKS AND ROMANS.*

Mestrius Plutarch lived between 45 and 120 A.D. and is the author of *Lives of the Noble Greeks and Romans*. The work, better known as *Parallel Lives* (many were ignoble), chronicles a pairing of historical characters for the purpose of moral illumination. The lives of Brutus, Julius Caesar and Mark Antony provided Shakespeare with the historical and, far more importantly, the character material for his play. Having said this, it is important to note that key elements, such as the specific orations, were Shakespeare's own inventions. He also substantially developed the characters of Portia, Calpurnia and Casca, as well as most of the minor characters.

JACQUES AMYOT AND SIR THOMAS NORTH

Shakespeare did not read Plutarch directly, but received the work in English from Thomas North, who worked from Jacques Amyot's popular French translation of Plutarch. The first edition of North's translation appeared in 1579 and was dedicated to Queen Elizabeth. A second edition followed in 1595, complete with new biographies.

Julius Caesar had political resonances for Queen Elizabeth.

ELIZABETH. *Julius Caesar,* likely the first play ever performed at the Globe Theater (1599), had political resonances for Shakespeare's patron, Queen Elizabeth I. The House of Commons, for example, kept an anxious eye on Elizabeth's growing power at a time when her reign was entering its final years. Like Caesar, Elizabeth had no heir (she named her second cousin James immediately before her death, much like Caesar named his grand-nephew Octavius). Perhaps most importantly, the members of the House and the English aristocracy worried that Elizabeth's death might plunge the nation into civil strife. During Elizabethan times, political commentary was risky at best; however, the dramatic arts could usually touch on social concerns without repercussion, so long as they were not overtly stated.

Oct. 45 B.C. - Return to Rome

Caesar returned to Rome, victorious over the sons of
Pompey, his one-time ally, turned enemy. He celebrated
his fifth triumph. A diadem was found on the statue of
Caesar and citizens called out, "King!" as he passed—some
were arrested. The tribunes responsible were called before
the senate by Caesar and stripped of their title. In
Shakespeare, the Lupercalia's juxtaposition to the episode
with the tribunes, makes the two events appear to be a
single celebration.

Feb. 15, 44 B.C. - Lupercalia

To mollify fears of his ambition, Caesar staged the refusal
of the diadem offered by Mark Antony. Shakespeare blurs
the story of the falling sickness from a report that, days
prior to the Lupercalia, Caesar did not rise for the senators
who presented him with honors (including making his
birthday, July 23, a national holiday). The breach of
protocol was eventually mitigated by Caesar through the
circulation of a story that he had the falling sickness and
therefore could not stand.

Mar. 15, 44 B.C. - Assassination

The assassination took place in the portico exedra (the
rectangular meeting room of the columned walkway) of
the Theater of Pompey. Shakespeare blurs this location
with the Capitol, which was under repair for fire damage
at the time of Caesar's assassination. Antony's brilliant
oration was delivered five days later, on March 20. The
conspirators flight to Greece followed closely thereafter.

Nov. 43 B.C. - Second Triumvirate

After much civil conflict, the second triumvirate of
Octavius, Antony and Lepidus was confirmed by law
through the Lex Titia. The proscriptions followed. Some
senators were killed; others had their property confiscated.
Cicero was arrested on December 7, attempting to flee to
Greece. His head and hands were severed and placed on
display in the public marketplace.

Oct. 42 B.C. - Two Battles

The first battle took place on October 7 on the
plains at Philippi. The battle would have been a
draw (Brutus defeated Octavius, Antony
defeated Cassius) except for Cassius' suicide
after his fateful misinterpretation of the facts.
The second action, just two weeks later on
October 23, led to the suicide of Brutus and the
control of Rome by the new triumvirate.

Feb	Apr	Jun	Aug	Oct	Dec	Feb	Apr	Jun	Aug	Oct	Dec	Feb	Apr	Jun	Aug	Oct	Dec	Feb	Apr	Jun	Aug	Oct	Dec
		45 B.C.						44 B.C.						43 B.C.						42 B.C.			

The events in the play span three years.

COLLAPSE. Though seemingly a few days or weeks at most, the events in Shakespeare's *Julius Caesar* span a historical time frame of some three years. Shakespeare chose to collapse seven significant events from Roman history in the composition of his play: Caesar's fifth triumph, the following Lupercalia, the assassination, the funeral oration, the proscription, the consolidation at Sardis and the two battles at Philippi.

With the poignant dramatic juxtaposition, some audience members are left with the feeling that these events occurred in rapid succession—which they did not. The triumph and Lupercalia are separated by four months time; the Roman holiday and the assassination are separated by one month; the oration follows one week later; the assassination and the proscription are some twenty months distant (the largest gap); finally, the two actions at Philippi are nearly a year after that, each battle being separated by about two weeks.

① CAESAR'S HOME
His home was in the Roman Forum, or marketplace, near the headquarters of the Pontifex Maximus (Caesar's religious title). Caesar traveled by litter in the company of Decius, who convinced him that Calpurnia's dream was a good omen and that the Senate planned to offer him the crown.

② CAESAR'S ASSASSINATION
Caesar arrived at the portico of the Theater of Pompey, where the Senate often met (Shakespeare confuses its identity with the Capitol). In the back of the theater jutted a rectangular meeting room. There, at the base of Pompey's statue, Caesar was killed.

③ THE CAPITOL BUILDING
The Capitol proper was under renovation at the time of Caesar's assassination and could not be used by the senate. Its confusion with the Theater of Pompey was a common misperception in medieval and renaissance times.

Rectangular curia (meeting room) adorned with Pompey's statue

Theater   Portico (columned walkway)

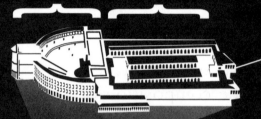

DETAIL OF POMPEY'S THEATER

② Theater of Pompey

Capitol ③

ROMAN FORUM ①

ROME

TIBER RIVER

Temple of Concord

Old Senate/Public Assembly and Speaker's platform (demolished)

Prison

Hall of Records

Commercial/Judicial Hall

Historic Pond

Caesar's headquarters and adjoining home

Temple of Saturn

Commercial/Judicial Hall (under construction)

New speaker's platform (under construction)

Temple of Castor and Pollux

Temple of Vesta

DETAIL OF ROMAN FORUM — 44 B.C.

40 kilometers
25 miles

Caesar was not killed in the Capitol.

CAPITOL. One of the seven hills of ancient Rome, Capitoline Hill, comprised the historic and religious heart of the city, housing important buildings, such as the temple of Jupiter and the Tabularium, the state civic archives. The Capitol was the location of the senate meetings, although alternative locations were often chosen for various reasons.

THEATER. The Theater of Pompey—the largest theater in the world at the time of Caesar—stood farther from the Forum. Since fire had damaged the Capitol, on March 15, 44 B.C., Julius Caesar called a meeting of the senate at the theater. The exedra of the portico, decorated with a statue of Pompey, was the actual site of the assassination. Caesar is said to have died at the foot of his rival's statue. Shakespeare blurs the two locations of the Capitol and Pompey' Theater, a common medieval and renaissance misunderstanding. He is correct in his reference to the statue and "Pompey's porch (portico)," but incorrectly refers to the site of the assassination as "the Capitol."